Neil Woodward

The Tyndale New Testament Commentaries *2001*

General Editor:
THE REV. CANON LEON MORRIS, M.Sc., M.Th., Ph.D.

COLOSSIANS
AND PHILEMON

For
Richard Gorrie
and
Lori Parisi

THE EPISTLES OF PAUL TO THE COLOSSIANS AND TO PHILEMON

AN INTRODUCTION AND COMMENTARY

by

N. T. WRIGHT, M.A., D. Phil.

Canon Theologian of Westminster Abbey

INTER-VARSITY PRESS

Inter-Varsity Press
38 De Montfort Street, Leicester LE1 7GP, England
Email: ivp@uccf.org.uk
World Wide Web: www.ivpbooks.com

© Nicholas Thomas Wright 1986

First published 1986
Reprinted 1999, 2000

British Library Cataloguing in Publication Data

Wright N. T.
  The Epistles of Paul to the Colossians and to
  Philemon: an introduction and commentary. —
  (Tyndale New Tastament commentaries)
  1. Bible. N.T. Colossians — Commentaries
  2. Bible. N.T. Philemon — Commentaries
  I. Title   II. Series
  227′.707   BS2715.3

ISBN 0-85111-881-X

Set in Palatino
Typeset in Great Britain by Parker Typesetting Service, Leicester
Printed and bound in Great Britain by Creative Print and Design (Wales), Ebbw Vale.

Inter-Varsity Press is the publishing division of the Universities and Colleges Christian Fellowship (formerly the Inter-Varsity Fellowship), a student movement linking Christian Unions in universities and colleges throughout Great Britain, and a member movement of the International Fellowship of Evangelical Students. For information about local and national activities write to UCCF, 38 De Montfort Street, Leicester LE1 7GP, Email: ivp@uccf.org.uk, or visit the UCCF website at http://www.uccf.org.uk.

GENERAL PREFACE

The original *Tyndale Commentaries* aimed at providing help for the general reader of the Bible. They concentrated on the meaning of the text without going into scholarly technicalities. They sought to avoid 'the extremes of being unduly technical or unhelpfully brief'. Most who have used the books agree that there has been a fair measure of success in reaching that aim.

Times, however, change. A series that has served so well for so long is perhaps not quite as relevant as when it was first launched. New knowledge has come to light. The discussion of critical questions has moved on. Bible-reading habits have changed. When the original series was commenced it could be presumed that most readers used the Authorized Version and one could make one's comments accordingly, but this situation no longer obtains.

The decision to revise and up-date the whole series was not reached lightly, but in the end it was thought that this is what is required in the present situation. There are new needs, and they will be better served by new books or by a thorough up-dating of the old books. The aims of the original series remain. The new commentaries are neither minuscule nor unduly long. They are exegetical rather than homiletic. They do not discuss all the critical questions, but none is written without an awareness of the problems that engage the attention of New Testament scholars. Where it is felt that formal consideration should be given to such questions, they are discussed in the Introduction and sometimes in Additional Notes.

But the main thrust of the commentaries is not critical. These books are written to help the non-technical reader to understand his Bible better. They do not presume a knowledge of Greek, and all Greek words discussed are transliterated; but the authors have the Greek text before them and their comments are made on the basis of the originals. The authors are free to choose their own modern translation, but are asked to bear in mind the variety of translations in current use.

The new series of *Tyndale Commentaries* goes forth, as the former series did, in the hope that God will graciously use these books to help the general reader to understand as fully and clearly as possible the meaning of the New Testament.

LEON MORRIS

CONTENTS

AUTHOR'S PREFACE

I well remember my first meeting with a biblical commentary. I was eighteen years old at the time, and was asked to lead a Bible Study group of six or eight contemporaries. The book we were to study was the letter to the Colossians, and the commentary which was lent to me was that by H. M. Carson, in the *Tyndale* series. It was just what I needed: lucid, informative, stimulating. I little thought then that I would one day be asked to write the volume that would replace it; and, when that invitation came, I accepted with a sense of gratitude, hoping that I might be able to do for another generation what Carson had done for me.

Study of Paul in general, and of Colossians in particular, has moved on by leaps and bounds in the last twenty years, and in starting again from scratch to work on the text I have tried to take account of what has been thought and written in the intervening period. This means, among other things, that I have made use of several works that, due to the different designs of various series, are able to include a wealth of technical detail that is outside the scope of this book: I think particularly of the commentaries of Lohse, Schweizer, O'Brien and (on Philemon) Stuhlmacher. I have frequently found, however, that older writers such as Lightfoot, Abbott and Williams still have a rich contribution to make, and are in no way superseded by more modern studies.

My debt to Professors G. B. Caird and C. F. D. Moule extends far beyond my grateful use of their respective commentaries. Both of them have given generously of their wisdom and friendship and have helped me to understand not only the New Testament but the very nature of Christian scholarship. There

9

are no words to express my sadness at George Caird's untimely death, which took place just after I had written the first draft of this preface. I had been looking forward eagerly to his comments on what I had written, and can now only guess at what they might have been. If this book reflects in any small way the academic rigour which he practised and taught, and the excitement which I always felt in exploring the New Testament under his guidance, I shall be proud.

Faced with the choice of basing the commentary on either the Revised Standard Version or the New International Version, I chose the latter, not because it is necessarily better but because, in my recent experience, a great many Christians have begun to use it. I have ventured to say from time to time where in my opinion its generally fine rendering of Paul could be improved. One of the good things about the plethora of modern translations currently available is that, by their very differences, they force readers of the Bible to ask searching questions about what the original text actually said. It seems to me, in this context, that the purpose of a commentary is (ultimately) to answer such questions by giving the text back to the reader uncluttered by a mass of glosses. To that end, this book has two aims: first, to clear up potential ambiguities or obscurities, so that the reader is able to hear, as nearly as possible, what the text itself says; second, to open the reader's eyes to see the text, and those parts of Paul's thought which it reflects, as a whole, over and above the mass of detail. In order to achieve these objects, I have not hesitated to give my own interpretation of several major questions which are raised by the text itself. All interpreters need to arrive at some position or other from which they can survey the land before them, and I hope that those who have accustomed themselves to looking at Colossians from other angles will at least try to see it from this perspective and assess whether it makes any more sense.

I was once accused in print of being naive for having written some positive remarks about the church. I am as well aware as anyone else of the weaknesses of the modern Western church. But I have persisted in holding to, and expounding, Paul's view (as it seems to me) of the church as the people of the new age. That I am still happy to do this is in large measure a tribute to the church within whose fellowship much of this book has been written. The Anglican Diocese of Montreal, and within it the parish of Hudson, Quebec, and the Diocesan Theological College, have shown me that it does indeed make sense to speak and write of the church as a loving and supportive community. In particular, two groups of enthusiastic lay people (one at Christ Church Cathedral in Montreal, and one in Hudson) listened to the substance of the book as a series of lectures, and offered a good deal of valuable support and comment. My colleagues Brian Walsh and Cathy Hird read the whole book as it came off the word processor, and gave me a great deal of help and constructive criticism. Our librarians at McGill, and those at l'Université de Montréal, have made my load considerably lighter, as has Mrs Darlene Fowler-Churchill by helping me learn how to process my words on a computer instead of typing them. The staff and editors of the Inter-Varsity Press have been patient in waiting for this book and shrewd in their handling of it. Dr Leon Morris has been the source of both considerable encouragement and wise criticism. I am grateful to them all, and hereby absolve them from any implication in the weaknesses which, despite their best efforts, this work still contains.

The book is dedicated to two remarkable people who, in their different ways, have helped me to see in practice, to understand, and to experience what Paul was talking about. It was Richard Gorrie who, nearly twenty years ago, put into my hands Carson's commentary on Colossians, and who thus, and in countless other ways, pointed me in the direction which led to the present task. It was Lori Parisi whose wise help and counsel ensured that I got on and finished it. The book belongs, in several important senses, to them as much as to me. To my parents and children, I owe a great debt (not least to my son Julian, for helping me with the map): to my dear wife, a debt greater still.

N. T. WRIGHT

CHIEF ABBREVIATIONS

AV   The Authorized (or King James') Version, 1611.
BAGD   *A Greek-English Lexicon of the New Testament and Other
            Early Christian Literature* (trans. of W. Bauer,
            Griechisch-Deutsches Wörterbuch), ed. by William F.
            Arndt and F. Wilbur Gingrich; second ed. revised
            and augmented by F. Wilbur Gingrich and F. W.
            Danker (University of Chicago Press, 1979).
BDF   F. Blass and A. Debrunner, *A Greek Grammar of the
            New Testament and Other Early Christian Literature*,
            trans. and revised by Robert W. Funk (Cambridge
            University Press, 1961).
Eng. Tr.   English translation.
EVV   English versions.
ExpT   *Expository Times.*
Ign.   Ignatius, letters of: *Eph., Ephesians; Rom., Romans;
            Philad., Philadelphinas; Pol., Polycarp.*
JB   The Jerusalem Bible, 1966.
JBL   *Journal of Biblical Literature.*
JSNT   *Journal for the Study of the New Testament.*
JTS   *Journal of Theological Studies.*
LXX   The Septuagint (pre-Christian Greek version of the
            Old Testament).
NEB   The New English Bible: Old Testament, 1970; New
            Testament, ²1970.
NIV   The Holy Bible: New International Version: Old
            Testament, 1978; New Testament, ²1978.
NTS   *New Testament Studies.*

OCD   *Oxford Classical Dictionary*, ed. M. Cary *et al.* (Oxford University Press, 1949).

RSV   The Revised Standard Version: Old Testament, 1952; New Testament, ^{2}1971.

SBL   Society of Biblical Literature.

BIBLIOGRAPHY

I. PRIMARY SOURCES

Novum Testamentum Graece, 26th edn, ed. K. Aland, M. Black, C. M. Martini, B. M. Metzger, A. Wikgren (Deutsche Bibelstiftung, 1979).

The Greek New Testament, 3rd edn, ed. K. Aland, M. Black, C. M. Martini, B. M. Metzger, A. Wikgren (United Bible Societies, 1975).

The Qumran Scrolls are cited according to the abbreviations listed in G. Vermes, *The Dead Sea Scrolls: Qumran in Perspective* (Collins, 1977), pp. 45–86, and may be found in English in G. Vermes, *The Dead Sea Scrolls in English*, 2nd edn (Penguin, 1975) (cited as 'Vermes').

The Pseudepigrapha are cited from the translations in J. H. Charlesworth (ed.), *The Old Testament Pseudepigrapha*, vol. 1: *Apocalyptic Literature and Testaments* (Doubleday, 1983).

The Septuagint is cited according to the edition of A. Rahlfs (Württembergische Bibelanstalt, 1935).

The Apostolic Fathers, Philo and Josephus are all cited according to the *Loeb Classical Library* editions (respectively, 1912–13, 1929–53 and 1926–65).

II. COMMENTARIES ON COLOSSIANS AND/OR PHILEMON

Commentaries in this list are cited by author's name only.

T. K. Abbott, *A Critical and Exegetical Commentary on the Epistles to*

14

the Ephesians and to the Colossians (*International Critical Commentaries*, T. & T. Clark, 1897).

E. K. Simpson and F. F. Bruce, *Commentary on the Epistles to the Ephesians and the Colossians* (*New International Commentary*, Marshall, Morgan & Scott/Eerdmans, 1957) (cited as 'Bruce').

G.B. Caird, *Paul's Letters from Prison (Ephesians, Philippians, Colossians, Philemon) in the Revised Standard Version: Introduction and Commentary* (Oxford University Press, 1976).

J. Calvin, *The Epistles of Paul the Apostle to the Galatians, Ephesians, Philippians and Colossians*, tr. T. H. L. Parker, ed. D. W. and T. F. Torrance (Eerdmans, 1965).

J. Calvin, *The Second Epistle of Paul the Apostle to the Corinthians, and the Epistles to Timothy, Titus and Philemon*, tr. T.A. Smail, ed. D. W. and T. F. Torrance (Eerdmans, 1964).

M. Dibelius, *An die Kolosser, Epheser: an Philemon*, revised by H. Greeven (Mohr, 1953).

J. Gnilka, *Der Kolosserbrief* (Herder, 1980).

J. L. Houlden, *Paul's Letters From Prison: Philippians, Colossians, Philemon and Ephesians* (Penguin, 1970).

G. Johnston, *Ephesians, Philippians, Colossians and Philemon* (*Century Bible*, new series, Nelson, 1967).

J. B. Lightfoot, *St. Paul's Epistles to the Colossians and to Philemon*, 2nd edn (Macmillan, 1876).

E. Lohse, *A Commentary on the Epistles to the Colossians and to Philemon*, Eng. Tr. (Fortress, 1971).

R. C. Lucas, *The Message of Colossians and Philemon: Fullness and Freedom* (*The Bible Speaks Today*, Inter-Varsity Press, 1980).

R. P. Martin, *Colossians and Philemon* (*New Century Bible*, Oliphants, 1974).

B. M. Metzger, *A Textual Commentary on the Greek New Testament* (United Bible Societies, 1971).

C. F. D. Moule, *The Epistles of Paul the Apostle to the Colossians and to Philemon* (*Cambridge Greek Testament*, Cambridge University Press, 1968).

S. C. Neill, *Paul to the Colossians* (*World Christian Books*, Lutterworth, 1963).

P. T. O'Brien, *Colossians and Philemon* (Word, 1982).

E. Schweizer, *The Letter to the Colossians: A Commentary*, Eng. Tr. (SPCK, 1982).

P. Stuhlmacher, *Der Brief an Philemon* (Benziger/Neukirchener, 1975).

M. R. Vincent, *A Critical and Exegetical Commentary on the Epistles to the Philippians and to Philemon* (*International Critical Commentaries*, T. & T. Clark, 1897).

A. L. Williams, *The Epistles of Paul the Apostle to the Colossians and to Philemon* (*Cambridge Greek Testament*, Cambridge University Press, 1907).

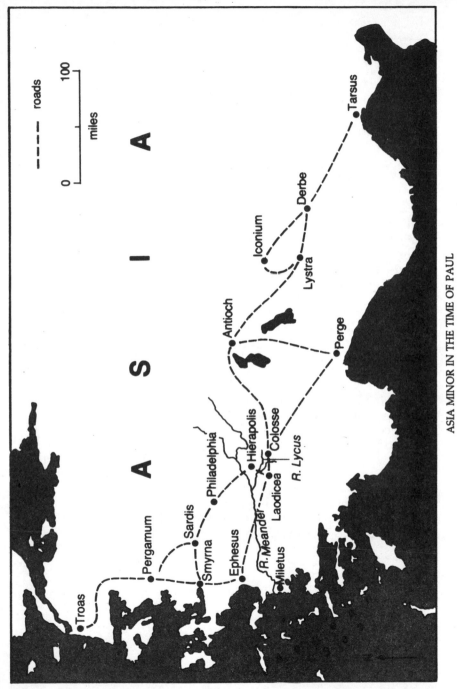

ASIA MINOR IN THE TIME OF PAUL

17

With you is Wisdom, she who knows your works,
she who was present when you made the world;
she understands what is pleasing in your eyes
and what agrees with your commandments . . .

She will guide me prudently in my undertakings
and protect me by her glory.
Then all I do will be acceptable,
I shall govern your people justly
and shall be worthy of my father's throne.
   Wisdom 9:9, 11–12 (Jerusalem Bible)

O loving Wisdom of our God!
 When all was sin and shame,
A second Adam to the fight
 And to the rescue came.
      John Henry Newman, *The Dream of Gerontius*

If anyone is in Christ – new creation!
The old is gone, the new has come . . .
God was in Christ reconciling the world to himself.
     2 Corinthians 5:17, 19 (author's own translation)

COLOSSIANS: INTRODUCTION

Colossians, one of the shortest of Paul's letters, is also one of the most exciting. Writing to a young church discovering what it was like to believe in Jesus Christ and to follow him, Paul shares their sense of wonder as he encourages them to explore the treasures of the gospel and to order their lives accordingly. There is, in fact, so much evocative language – talk about the gospel, about Jesus Christ, about holiness, about the church – that it is easy to lose track of the overall thread of the letter and merely to pick out a few details. But if the details are worth having, the letter as a whole is even more so. It is not a miscellaneous collection of 'helpful thoughts'. It is a particular letter written to a particular congregation at one point in its (very early) history. To believe, in fact, that Colossians is inspired Scripture is to believe that God intended to say just these things to this church – and in so doing to address, somehow, the church as a whole.

But what were these things? And why did they need saying? And what relevance may it all have for a different church in a different place and time? Ultimately, these questions can be answered only as we go along through the book. But certain preliminary points can be made at this stage.

I. THE SHAPE OF THE LETTER

Colossians, like many books, and for that matter like most symphonies, plays or poems, is not the sort of work that can be simply split up into successive units, like the separate inches marked on a ruler. A simple analysis of contents is therefore not sufficient to show what the book is really about. It is more like a flower, growing from a small bud to a large bud and then gradually opening up to reveal, layer upon layer, the petals that had all along been hidden inside. We may briefly observe this unfolding process, as follows.

After the initial greeting (1:1–2) comes Paul's great prayer of thanksgiving for the church at Colosse (1:3–8), which turns into intercession on their behalf (1:9–23). He prays, basically, that the young church may learn how to thank God for what he has done for them in Christ. Out of this there grows Paul's initial statement of his purpose in writing (1:24 – 2:5): the Christian maturity he has sought in prayer on the Colossians' behalf he is now working to produce by writing to them. With this the bud is opened fully, revealing the great central section of the letter, which itself unfolds in the same way. Paul begins with a pregnant pair of verses (2:6–7), whose basic command is to 'walk in Christ'; he then attacks certain teachings that would prevent the Colossians from doing this in the full, mature way he longs to see (2:8–19). Central to his appeal is the fact that Christians have already 'been buried and raised with Christ' (2:12), and this idea unfolds in turn (2:20 – 3:4) to give more detailed instructions. The double-edged appeal ('since you died with Christ . . . since you have been raised with Christ . . .', 2:20; 3:1) is finally amplified into the two paragraphs 3:5–11 and 3:12–17, concluding with the command (3:17) to do all things in the name of the Lord Jesus, giving thanks to God the Father through him – which is, more or less, the sum and substance of the whole appeal. But Paul's picture of the life of the new age is not one of generalizations. He applies it in detail to two areas of life, the home (3:18 – 4:1) and the world (4:2–6). The body of the letter thus concludes where it began, with a picture of God at work, through the gospel, in the world (see 1:3–8). In the final section (4:7–18) Paul conveys greetings, from fellow-workers who are with him and to other churches in the neighbourhood of Colosse. This closing section serves as a reminder that we are dealing not simply with abstract truth but with a flesh-and-blood letter, which must be handled as such if it is to yield its secrets.

Two points about this outline (which is set out diagrammatically on pp. 44f. below) should be noted. First, Paul is not writing what we might think of as a standard theological treatise, beginning with 'doctrine' and ending with 'ethics' or 'practical teaching'.[1] For him, all is doctrine, all is practice, all is worship, because all is Christ. Secondly, therefore, it should be observed that virtually every section and sub-section in the main body of the letter could be accurately summed up with reference to Christ himself. This indicates an important truth about Colossians: its driving force comes from that which is stated in 1:15–20. The main reason why the Colossians should give thanks to God is because of Jesus Christ; if they do this with full knowledge and understanding about who he is and what he has achieved, everything else will fall into place.

II. THE CIRCUMSTANCES OF WRITING

Treating Colossians as a real letter means asking when, where and why it was written – and, indeed, by whom, since, though it purports to be by Paul (1:1; 4:18 and by frequent implication), not all scholars have been convinced that it was written by the apostle himself. It is possible to argue the case for Pauline authorship in a compelling fashion, but to do so here would be to duplicate the work of other recent writers.[2] I prefer to come at the matter by a different route, asking first why the letter seems to have been written and then, in the light of the answer we receive, drawing conclusions about its authorship, date and location.

a. Colosse

The recipients of the letter were the members of a reasonably young church in Colosse, a town on the banks of the river Lycus in south-east Asia Minor (modern Turkey): see the map on page 17. It was neither a large nor an important town, though it had formerly been both; it had been upstaged by its near neighbours

---

[1]Against, *e.g.*, Lohse, pp.3 f., Schweizer, p.15.   [2]See, recently, O'Brien, pp.xli-xlix.

Laodicea, ten miles away, and Hierapolis, six miles beyond that.[1] The letter indicates that Paul, who seems to have concentrated on major centres of population, had not visited the town himself: the Christian community there owed its origin under God to his fellow-worker Epaphras, who had brought news of Christ from Paul to Colosse and then news of a new church from Colosse to Paul (1:7–8).

What we know of the religious life of towns like Colosse is based on inference from evidence relating to that part of Asia Minor in general and from Paul's writings in particular. (Since Colosse itself has not been excavated, there is no archaeological evidence available for saying what local cults may have flourished, or how many Jews had made their home there.) Paul alludes several times to the pagan past of his converts (1:12–13, 21, 27; 2:13; 3:5–7),[2] and it is likely that Colosse had its fair share of the variegated religious practices which characterized the ancient Near East at this time. In this society the old gods of classical Greek culture still had their adherents, as did the 'mystery-religions' which promised entry to a secret, higher world for those who submitted to the proper initiation. With the passage of time and the movement of people from one area to another, the lines between different cults and religious ideas could get blurred, and the phenomenon known as 'syncretism' – the mixing of religious ideas and practices from a wide range of sources – became quite common.[3]

At the same time, as Acts 15:21 puts it, Moses had representatives in every city. Each town would have one or more synagogues, and it has been calculated that around this period the adult male Jewish population in the neighbouring area of Laodicea was about eleven thousand. (Rome at this time had between forty and fifty thousand Jews, out of a total population of around a million, excluding slaves.)[4] We know from a variety of sources that Judaism, in one form or another, was attractive

---

[1]Further details in F.F. Bruce, *Paul: Apostle of the Free Spirit* (in the U.S. *Paul: Apostle of the Heart Set Free*) (Paternoster/Eerdmans, 1977), pp.407 ff.; O'Brien, pp.xxvi f.

[2]See O'Brien, pp.xxviii f., citing Moule, p.29.

[3]For all this, see now the full treatment in H. Koester, *Introduction to the New Testament*, Eng. Tr. (Fortress, 1982), vol. 1, pp.164–203.

[4]For Laodicea, see O'Brien, p.xxvii; for Rome, see G. La Piana, 'Foreign Groups in Rome During the First Centuries of the Empire', *Harvard Theological Review* 20, 1927, pp.183–403.

to many pagans weary of the confused, often amoral religion of their own background, and it is likely that Christianity would make a similar impression on pagan hearers. It would therefore be easy (as we know from Galatians) for young converts to Christianity to become muddled, and to imagine that, having become Christians, they must complete the process by becoming Jews. It is this tendency that Paul is resolutely opposing in, for instance, Galatians, and in Philippians 3. It is my contention that a similar danger was the reason for the writing of Colossians, at least chapter 2. But this is a controversial claim, and must be advanced in various stages.

b. The problem of Colossians

Scholars have long held that Colossians was written to combat a particular danger within the young church. False teachers were inculcating spurious doctrines and practices, demoting Christ from his position of unique pre-eminence, and encouraging various dubious mystical and ascetic religious practices. But there is no agreement on the identity of these teachers or the nature of their teaching. Some suggest a pagan cult of one sort or another; others, some form of sectarian Judaism; others, an early form of gnosticism; others, a blend of some or all of these. Recently an attempt has been made to trace affinities between the Colossian heresy and the teaching of the Pythagorean philosophy.[1]

We cannot here discuss each of these solutions, let alone the arguments surrounding them. The problem, in its essence, could be stated as follows. (a) There are clear Jewish elements in what Paul is opposing, and yet there are many things which look more pagan than Jewish – the actual worship of angels (2:18), and ascetic practices which appear to deny the importance of the created order (2:20ff.). (b) On the other hand, while much of what Paul is opposing can be fitted into an essentially

---

[1] See the surveys in F.O. Francis and W. Meeks, eds., *Conflict at Colosse* (SBL/Scholars' Press, 1975); O'Brien, pp.xxx-xli; Schweizer (who takes the 'Pythagorean' view), pp.125–134. Schweizer is wrong, incidentally, when he says that Caird 'posits a Jewish-Stoic movement' (p.126, n.1); Caird (pp.163 f.) discusses this possibility but does not recommend it.

non-Jewish framework, there are certain features (for instance, the reference to circumcision in 2:11) which remain obstinately and uniquely Jewish. No syncretistic religion has yet been discovered which had exactly this blend of things pagan and Jewish; nor is this a mere accident of our limited historical knowledge, since it is in fact difficult to conceive of even the possibility of such a blend. (c) The problem, therefore, is to find a hypothesis which will account for the polemic of Colossians both in outline and in detail. If, at the same time, such a hypothesis can help to explain the significance of the poem in 1:15–20, and of the particular form and content of the ethical exhortations in chapter 3, it will gain added strength.

c. The underlying solution: polemic against Judaism

The answer I wish to offer is essentially simple, but some of the supporting arguments involve more technical complexity than is appropriate in a volume such as this, and have been set out fully elsewhere.[1] What follows is therefore a summary of the essential points, some of which will be amplified further in the commentary.

Within the overall drift of the argument of the letter two features stand out: (a) the centrality of Christ throughout and (b) the emphasis, within chapter 2, on 2:11–12 and 2:13–15. The latter passages assert that the Colossian Christians have already been 'circumcised' and that God has dealt with the 'written code . . . that was against us'. I believe that these features are best explained on the assumption that Paul is warning the reader not to be taken in by the claims of Judaism, which would try (as in Acts 15:5) to persuade pagan converts to Christianity that their present position was incomplete. On the contrary, Paul declares: in Christ you have already been 'circumcised', and have been set free from any claim that the Jewish law might make on you. No-one must therefore attempt to exclude you from the inner circle of God's people (2:16, 18, 20). The master-stroke in Paul's argument is thus that he warns ex-pagans against Judaism by portraying Judaism itself as if it were just another pagan

---

[1] See my article, 'The problem of Colossians', forthcoming in *JTS*.

religion. It is a 'philosophy' (2:8), developed by human tradition (2:8, 22): and to follow it is to return to the same type of religion the new converts had recently abandoned. A good deal of chapter 2 in particular can therefore be understood as characteristically Pauline irony (see the commentary for details).

This hypothesis has three particular strengths.

i. The underlying view of Christ in the letter (set out particularly in 1:15–20) is that he has taken the position which Judaism assigned to the Jewish law. Having Christ, therefore, the new converts already possessed all they needed: Judaism had nothing more to offer them.

ii. A contrast with Judaism enables several passages in the letter to gain in significance. Paul's argument amounts to a redefinition of the cardinal Jewish doctrines of monotheism and election. With Christ at the centre, he presents a new view of God and his people. Thus (*e.g.*) in 1:12ff. Paul declares that the church has had its own 'exodus', and is the heir to the true promised land. In chapters 2 and 3 he stresses that the church already lives in the 'age to come' that Jews expected, and is therefore under no obligation to submit to regulations that were essentially a preparation for that age.

iii. This position enables us to understand the many parallels between Colossians and several other well-known Pauline passages, such as Galatians 3 – 4, Romans 7:1–6, Philippians 3:2ff., and particularly 2 Corinthians 3 – 5, which offer several very important parallels to Colossians.[1] In each of these passages, albeit in different ways according to context, Paul contrasts Judaism and the gospel of Jesus Christ in ways which cohere well with Colossians.

There are certain obvious problems with this position, which may be answered as follows.

i. It is true that Paul never here uses the word 'law' (*nomos*) or commandment (*entolē*), which feature prominently in some of his other discussions of Christianity and Judaism (*e.g.* Romans, Galatians).[2] But I shall argue in the commentary that (a) 2:13ff. is

---

[1] See the details in the article referred to in n.1, p.24, above.
[2] See E. Schweizer, 'Zur neueren Forschung am Kolosserbrief (seit 1970)' in *Theologische Berichte* 5, eds. J. Pfammatter and F. Furger (Zürich, 1976), pp.163–191, here at p.174; O'Brien, p.xxxi; Gnilka, pp.163 f.

best understood as an oblique reference to the Jewish law; (b) 1:15ff. is best taken as an ascription to Christ of the position some Jews gave to their law;[1] (c) the language used of Christ in 2:3 is almost certainly borrowed from 'terms used by Judaism concerning the law', so that Paul 'here substitutes Christ for the Law';[2] (d) the regulations referred to in 2:16 fit the Jewish law and nothing else. In addition, (e) 2 Corinthians 3 – 5 demonstrates that Paul is quite capable of mounting a full-dress argument about the old and new covenants in which the words 'law' and 'commandment' do not appear. Finally, and most importantly, (f) it is likely that Paul has avoided these key terms for a good reason: namely, that they still carry, for him, positive as well as negative connotations (see Rom. 3:31; 7:12, 16; 8:4, 7). In warning the Colossians against the present Jewish use of the law, he is not going to fall into the trap of denying the divine origin of the law itself.

ii. The things Paul is attacking (angel-worship, ascetic practices and 'philosophy') do not look particularly Jewish. This, indeed, is the basis of the usual alternative theories, which postulate some kind of syncretistic religion. But (a) several scholars have recently pointed out the close connection between the attack on angel-worship in 2:18 and various aspects of Judaism;[3] (b) it is easier to understand the references to asceticism (2:20–23) as contemptuous and ironic, and the close parallel with Mark 7:5ff. increases the probability that the target of the polemic is the Jewish law: (c) Philo and Josephus, Jewish writers of the first century, both use the word 'philosophy' to describe Judaism, or particular parties within it, to pagans,[4] and there is no reason why Paul should not have done the same –

[1] See M. D. Hooker, 'Were there False Teachers in Colossae?' in *Christ and Spirit in the New Testament: In Honour of Charles Francis Digby Moule*, eds. B. Lindars and S. S. Smalley (CUP, 1973), pp.315–331.

[2] O'Brien, p.96, citing Is. 33:5–6; 1 Baruch 3:15 – 4:1; Ecclus. 24:23 (this should perhaps have read 24:1–23); 2 Baruch 44:14; 54:13; and secondary literature.

[3] See further F. O. Francis, 'Humility and Angelic Worship in Col. 2:18', *Studia Theologica* 16, 1962, pp.109–134; C. C. Rowland, *The Open Heaven: A Study of Apocalyptic in Judaism and Early Christianity* (SPCK/Crossroad, 1982), especially ch. 4. Rowland (p.409) cites Col. 2:16ff. as 'evidence of a considerable degree of Jewish influence on the beliefs and practices of Christian communities in Asia Minor'.

[4] Philo *de Somn.* 2:127; *Leg. ad Gai.* 156, 245; *De Mut. Nom.* 223; *Omn. Prob. Lib.* 88; Jos. *Bell.* 2:119; *Ant.* 18:11. See also 4 Macc. 1:1; 5:10, 22; 7:7–9; and compare Schweizer, p.136, n.8.

particularly if his purpose here is precisely to describe Judaism as 'just another religion'.

My hypothesis, then, is that all the elements of Paul's polemic in Colossians make sense as a warning against Judaism. The way to maturity for the people of God does not lie in their becoming Jews, but rather in their drawing out, and applying to personal and communal life, the meaning of the death and resurrection of Jesus Christ. This means that those theories which find parallels to certain aspects of the Colossian 'situation' in gnosticism, mystery religions or other philosophies, such as Stoicism and Pythagoreanism, are not necessary.[1] Nor are they even sufficient: they fall by their own weight, since they fail completely to explain the passage about circumcision in 2:11ff., and the extremely Jewish appearance of 2:16ff.

If we thus place Colossians alongside Galatians and other passages in which Paul's polemic is aimed at Judaism, we see many clear parallels. But at the same time there are important differences. In Galatians Paul clearly faces a present and active opposing faction, and is seriously concerned lest his converts' faith be undermined. In Colossians his argument and tone suggest that the same is not true here. This has led at least one recent scholar to question whether there really were 'false teachers' in Colosse whose work and doctrine Paul was trying to undermine.[2] This suggestion finds additional support in, for instance, Paul's thanksgiving for the church and its faith (1:3–8), and particularly in his comment in 2:5 that they are in good order and that their faith in Christ is firm.

There is, in fact, nothing in the letter which *requires* us to postulate that Paul is opposing actual false teachers who were already infiltrating the church. The main emphasis of the letter is on Christian maturity. Paul knew well enough that his footsteps had been dogged, elsewhere in Asia Minor, by those offering a different sort of 'maturity', seeking to win over ex-pagan Christians to observance of the Jewish law. It is quite natural that he should issue such a warning in the course of his positive message, not merely because the danger might be

[1]See above, p.23, n.1. This criticism applies particularly to the elaborate theories of Martin and Schweizer. For discussion of the view of G. Bornkamm see Gnilka, pp.165 f.
[2]See Hooker, 'Were there False Teachers in Colosse?'

pressing at some future point, but because it enabled him to highlight, by contrast, the fundamental fact that Christians are members, in Christ, of the true people of God, the true humanity. To suggest, then, that there are opponents actually present in Colosse (however fashionable such suggestions may be) may well be to read too much between the lines. This does not mean, of course, that Paul's readers would have had difficulty in understanding what he was talking about. The fact of a large Jewish minority presence in the cities and towns of Asia Minor at this period would have meant that thoughtful ex-pagans would be quite capable of recognizing the target of Paul's polemic, even if they did not at once see all its subtleties.

Was Paul, then, envisaging an attempt by non-Christian Jews to persuade the converts to move lock, stock and barrel from the church to the synagogue? Or was he really more anxious about Christians who were attempting to combine allegiance to Christ with observance of the Jewish law – the militant 'Jewish Christians' whom we meet at various points in the New Testament (Acts 11:2–3; 15:5; Gal. 2:12; Tit. 1:10)? A decision here is difficult. It is by no means as clear as most commentators assume that the teaching Paul is opposing made room, officially, for Jesus Christ within its system. The one verse which might suggest this is 2:19; the attack is to be expected from people who, though claiming to belong to Christ, are not 'holding fast' to him as the head of the body, but are in fact allowing the Torah to take his supreme place. But the word usually translated 'holding fast' (*kratōn*) can not only mean 'holding on to', of something already grasped, but also 'grasping' of something one does not already hold. It could, therefore, refer to people who had never belonged to Christ at all (NIV 'he has lost connection with the Head' goes beyond the Greek). Furthermore, Paul's claim in Colossians is that, in clinging to the badge of circumcision and the ethical safety-net of the Jewish law, those who want to lure ex-pagan Christians into full synagogue membership are making a category mistake. They are trying to persuade those who have entered the new age to step back into the old. This criticism applies not so much (as in Galatians) to the 'Jewish Christian' position, but to Judaism itself.

This interpretation of Paul's polemic raises, of course, the question of whether Paul is, here and for that matter elsewhere, guilty of anti-Semitism or anti-Judaism.[1] Space forbids the full discussion that this question warrants, and I must simply summarize the fuller argument that could be made.[2] It is true that a caricature of Paul has dominated scholarship for a long time, in which he is opposed to all things Jewish simply because of their Jewishness, and in which he attacks Judaism for holding doctrines which, it now appears, were not held in quite that form at all. This picture has now been replaced in many scholarly circles by a new one, its mirror image, in which Paul has no (or next to no) critique of Judaism at all.[3] Somewhere between these two extremes lies the truth, and Colossians is in fact an important part of the relevant evidence for deciding the issue.

Where, then, does the truth lie? Paul believed that Jesus was the Messiah; that with Jesus' death and resurrection and the sending of the Holy Spirit the new covenant had been inaugurated (2 Cor. 3); that the people of Jesus Christ were the true people of God, the sole inheritors of the promises to Abraham (Gal. 3; Rom. 4); and that the gospel events provided a sharp critique of *all* humanity, Jews not excepted, and therefore a warning to Jew and Gentile alike to find salvation in Christ, the only place where it was available. This only makes Paul anti-Jewish to the extent that it also makes him 'opposed' to fallen humanity in general; but this 'opposition' is not one of hatred, but of concerned love (Rom. 9:1–5; 10:1–2; 2 Cor. 5:14–15; *etc.*). Paul makes no effort, as later anti-Semitism (including the *soi-disant* 'Christian' variety) has done on occasion, to argue that the synagogue, or Jewish customs and institutions, or Jewish people themselves, should logically cease to exist. He continued to attend synagogue.[4] He argues that Jews still have the right, and the chance, to hear the gospel, to believe in Jesus Christ, and so to be saved (Rom. 11:11–32, itself an argument against an incipient 'Christian' anti-Semitism which would argue that Jews

[1]See, *e.g.*, R. R. Ruether, *Faith and Fratricide: The Theological Roots of Anti-Semitism* (Seabury, 1974), pp.95–107. The often shrill tone of this book should not be allowed to deafen its readers to the many important points that it has to make.
[2]See now J. G. Gager, *The Origins of Anti-Semitism* (OUP, 1984).
[3]See, *e.g.*, K. Stendahl, *Paul Among Jews and Gentiles* (Fortress, 1976).
[4]See E. P. Sanders, *Paul, the Law and the Jewish People* (Fortress, 1983), p.192.

cannot now be saved).[1] If this be anti-Judaism, it is nothing for a Christian to be ashamed of. The only alternative is to deny that Jesus is the Messiah, that God raised him from the dead and so demonstrated that his death was the means of dealing with sin (1 Cor. 15:14, 17), that the Spirit of Jesus is the Holy Spirit of God, who brings into being the people of God of the 'new age'. Paul has hard words to say against those who deny these things, whether explicitly or (by their desire to combine Christianity with orthodox Judaism) implicitly. If Romans 9 – 11 is anything to go by, he would have had equally hard words to say against those who, in the name of the Jewish Messiah, persecute Jews or deny them their rights, including the right to practise their ancestral religion. There is no political programme concealed in Paul's theological polemic. If subsequent generations have turned it into such a programme, that is scarcely his fault. He knew the difference between church and state (Rom. 13:1–7), between the argument that Judaism is theologically obsolete as the way of salvation and the idea that it is the enemy of a 'Christian' state (and therefore to be eliminated).

Paul's critique of Judaism does not aim, as in the old caricature, at 'legalism', the supposed attempt to earn righteousness through good works. It aims at the position of national superiority which Judaism had thought to claim on the basis of God's choice of her. Observance of the Law, the national charter, was designed not to earn membership in the covenant but to embody and express it. For Paul, the gospel of the crucified and risen Messiah reveals that God has all along had a different end in view. National Israel, with her Law, was simply the preliminary stage in this plan, which always envisaged an eventual world-wide family.

---

[1] I have argued this position at length in ch. 4 of *The Messiah and the People of God: A Study in Pauline Theology with Particular Reference to the Argument of the Epistle to the Romans*, unpublished D. Phil. thesis (Oxford University, 1980). I do not think that Romans 11 refers either to a large-scale last-minute conversion of 'all Jews' (whatever that might mean) or to a way of salvation for Jews which is other than through faith in Jesus Christ. See too S. C. Neill, *Christian Faith and Other Faiths*, 2nd edn (Hodder/IVP, 1984), p.42.

III. AUTHORSHIP

But did Paul himself really write Colossians? So far we have
assumed that he did; but scholarly opinion is by no means
unanimous on the point. There is not even agreement on where
the weight of argument must lie if the issue is to be settled. Some
of those who doubt Colossians' authenticity build their case on
theology, saying that the style of the letter does not provide a
clear enough indication.[1] Others, happy to say that the theology
of the letter is substantially Pauline, think that the style alone
forces us to say that someone other than Paul wrote it.[2] This
suggests, actually, that neither the style nor the theology is as
decisive in mounting an argument against authenticity as some
have suggested. More recent work has shown that an excellent
case for Pauline authorship can still be made out.[3] I wish here
simply to focus on certain points which further advance this case.

First, there are some general problems with attributing Colossians to someone other than Paul. Putting the letter in the
post-Pauline period, as has been the fashion in some circles,
makes the personal allusions, and particularly those of chapter
4, very hard to explain.[4] But making it contemporary with Paul,
and yet assigning it to a different hand, as Schweizer does (he
suggests Timothy), is to solve one (supposed) problem by creating another. We know nothing whatever of Timothy's literary
capabilities, and examples from other areas of human art (such
as the completion, by Süssmaier, of Mozart's *Requiem*) do not
encourage us to suppose that creative genius can be 'caught'
even by long familiarity with the master and his work. In particular, we may well wonder whether anyone other than Paul
himself would have been so bold with his irony, so characteristically terse and pregnant in his theological statements and Old
Testament allusions. Deliberate imitations – as, if not by Paul,

[1]*E.g.* Lohse, pp.89–91.   [2]*E.g.* Schweizer, pp.18 f.   [3]O'Brien, pp.xli–xlix.
[4]Leaving aside the whole question of pseudonymity, *i.e.* whether the practice of writing
books in someone else's name was as widespread in the early church as is sometimes
thought, and if so, what the criteria might be for deciding whether a particular work was an
example of this. On this matter see the discussion (in relation to 2 Peter, though the
argument admits of wider application) of J. A. T. Robinson, *Redating the New Testament*
(SCM Press, 1976), pp.186 ff.

we must suppose Colossians to be – are usually wooden, self-conscious things, not flowing and vibrant as this letter is.

This leads us to considerations of style. It is true that there are several details of verbal usage which make Colossians stand out just a little from the undoubted Pauline letters.[1] But almost all of these, when examined, turn out to be of little significance, as Lohse admits.[2] Each epistle has words that are peculiar to it, so that finding such words in Colossians tells us very little. And all the supposed oddities of wording can in fact be paralleled from the other letters.[3] The style of argument, it is true, is not the same as that in Romans or Galatians, where question-and-answer dialogue, and detailed treatment of Old Testament passages, make up a good part of the argument. But the other letters indicate that this was by no means the only style that Paul could adopt. And in fact Colossians does appear typically Pauline in other stylistic respects. Themes are stated briefly or poetically, and then developed further: in 1:15–20 and 2:6ff., for instance, we find a very similar pattern (poetic statement, followed later by detailed application) to Philippians 2:6–11 and 3:2ff., and other similar passages.

The real weight of the argument against Pauline authorship lies, I believe, on the question of theology.[4] Here again the case is not as strong as it is sometimes made to seem. To begin with, a general point. The popular idea that the Captivity Epistles (our two letters, with Ephesians and Philippians) show a more developed, and hence later, theological position than do the (supposedly) earlier ones rests on a mistake. We are able to chart changes in (say) Calvin's mind by studying the differences

[1]Details in Lohse, pp.84–88; more fully in W. Bujard, *Stilanalytische Untersuchungen zum Kolosserbrief als Beitrag zur Methodik von Sprachvergleichen* (Vandenhoek und Ruprecht, 1973).

[2]Lohse, p.91.

[3]Lohse considers *ho estin* (1:24; 3:14 and perhaps 1:27 – there are MS variants in each instance) to be an exception. But there are parallels for this kind of explanatory phrase in Gal. 3:16 (*hos estin*; some MSS have *ho estin*); 2 Thes. 3:17; and Eph. 1:14; 5:5; 6:17. Parallels from 2 Thessalonians and Ephesians will not of course impress those who consider those letters, too, inauthentic. But the verse in Galatians shows that this kind of phrase is perfectly possible for Paul.

[4]Schweizer comes and goes on this question. On the one hand he claims (pp.18 f.) that the author follows Paul 'completely in vocabulary and theological concepts'; but in the commentary itself he frequently attempts to drive a wedge between the theologies of Paul and of Colossians.

between successive editions of the *Institutes*, and it might appear easy to do the same with Paul and his letters. But this appearance is deceptive. The greater historical distance between us and him; the very small amount of relevant comparative material; the 'occasional' nature of the letters – all these warn us to be on our guard against over-hasty conclusions. Artists, writers and composers by no means always show a unilinear development in their work. And when, in fact, we enquire where (other than with Ephesians) Colossians finds its closest ties, we receive a bewildering variety of answers. The theology of Colossians does not evidence a uniformly 'late' view, but links itself to major themes in almost all of Paul's other letters. The Christology fits well with Philippians 2:6–11; 1 Corinthians 8:6; 2 Corinthians 4:4; 8:9; while the ironic critique of Judaism, and the argument for seeing Christians as the true covenant people, belong with Romans 2:17–29; Philippians 3:2–11 and 2 Corinthians 3, and with Galatians as a whole. The references to the church as Christ's body (1:18, 24; 2:19) should not be seen as a radical departure from 1 Corinthians 12 and Romans 12 (Christ as the whole body, not just the head) but as different uses of the same underlying metaphor. Finally, the pregnant and difficult verse about suffering (1:24) can be understood only if we line it up with 2 Corinthians 1:3–11; 4:7–18 and Romans 8:17–25. The simplest hypothesis by far is to see all these letters as proceeding from the same pen in the same period of six or eight years. They all reflect not only the needs and problems of the individual churches to which they were addressed, but also the same overall theological position, however many different expressions it may find.

Colossians does not, it is true, mention the doctrine of justification. (It is, however, frequently implicit, for instance in 3:10–13.) But behind this difference (which only applies, anyway, to Romans, Galatians and Philippians 3:2ff.) the similarities with the other letters are very striking. The real centre of Paul's thought, as of his life, is not justification, but that which underlies it and gives it its polemical cutting edge, namely, the crucified and risen Jesus, seen as the revelation in action of the one creator God, the God of Abraham, appearing on the stage of history to fulfil his purposes and promises and to create for himself a world-wide people. The doctrine of justification, vital though it is, is but one way of stating this central truth: it cannot be used as the measuring-rod of Paul's whole thought. That position belongs to Christology: and that, arguably, is what Colossians is all about. That this in no way relativizes justification, or subordinates it to other doctrines in a way which tames or muzzles its polemical nature, should be clear from my treatment of 2:6–23.

There is therefore no need to reject the Pauline authorship of Colossians, nor to imagine that its authenticity must be defended by the hypothesis that Paul wrote it when he was older, more settled and mellow, than he had been when writing Romans or Galatians. Indeed, that view hardly fits 2:6–23, or for that matter Philippians 3:2ff. Colossians can be seen as simply one more example of that vivid and brilliant theological writing which characterizes, uniquely, everything Paul himself wrote.

IV. DATE AND PLACE OF WRITING

Finally, then, we must consider when and where the letter was written. The reference to imprisonment (4:3, which refers to the author's being 'in chains' – always assuming, as most do, that this is not to be taken metaphorically) has linked the letter not only with Philemon (see below, p. 191) and Ephesians (*cf.* Eph. 6:20), but also with Philippians, where literal imprisonment is brought into the explicit argument of the letter (Phil. 1:12–30). These four letters have therefore frequently been grouped together as 'letters from prison', and all four may well have been written from the same prison at about the same time. The strong ties of Colossians with Ephesians and Philemon support this, though Philippians does not so obviously bear, as one might say, the same Opus number. If we try to use these data in order to tie down at least Colossians and Philemon (we will discuss presently the problems raised by the special relationship between our letter and Ephesians), we find at least three possible periods of imprisonment: those in Ephesus (inferred from 2 Cor. 1:8; 1 Cor. 15:32), Caesarea (Acts 24:27) and Rome (Acts 28:16ff.). (That there were periods of imprisonment other than those recorded in Acts we know from the references in 2 Cor. 6:5 and 11:23.)

Arguments for each of these three cities as the location of some or all of the prison epistles have been advanced by different scholars with skill and ingenuity, and the issue remains finely balanced. (Thus, for instance, the references to the praetorian guard and to Caesar's household, in Phil. 1:13 and 4:22, could indicate Rome; but they could equally well suggest the Roman garrison at Ephesus or Caesarea.) Colossians has, however, increasingly given me the impression of a letter to a church which, very young in the faith, needs to be strengthened, informed about what has actually happened to its members in their becoming Christians, taught how to pursue Christian maturity, and warned against a threat most dangerous for those only recently converted from paganism. If this is correct – and such a hypothesis is of course incapable of cast-iron proof – it would suggest Ephesus as the location. During Paul's imprisonment, his fellow-workers have been busy on his behalf (1:7, if the reading 'on our behalf' is correct). Among them is Epaphras, who has preached the gospel in Colosse (a little over a hundred miles inland) and the surrounding area, and who has returned to Paul with news of the new church there. This fits well with the letter to Philemon. Despite some contrary suggestions,[1] I believe that it is much more likely that Onesimus would have gone to Paul in Ephesus than in Rome, and much easier for Paul both to send him back and perhaps (if Phm. 14 is so to be understood) to request that he be returned to him again. Onesimus was after all a runaway slave, with a price on his head; however good the Roman roads were, a double and perhaps a triple journey between Rome and Colosse would be asking a lot. Paul himself did not find it that easy to get to Rome. In addition, it seems unlikely that, having seen Rome as a staging-post on the way to Spain (Rom. 15:22–29), Paul would be hoping to visit Philemon soon after his impending release.[2]

[1]E.g. C. H. Dodd, *New Testament Studies*, 2nd Edn (Manchester University Press, 1967), pp.94 f.
[2]See Phm. 22, and the commentary on that verse. For a full statement of the argument for Ephesus, see G. S. Duncan, *St. Paul's Ephesian Ministry* (Hodder, 1929), and his subsequent articles in *ExpT* 67, 1955–6, pp.163–166; *NTS* 3, 1956–7, pp.211–218, and *NTS* 5, 1958–9,

The personal details in 4:7–17 fit well with this hypothesis. Mark, at present with Paul, may be about to pay the Colossians a visit (4:10) – quite unlikely if he is in Rome or Caesarea. Tychicus and Onesimus will tell the Colossians 'everything that is happening here' (4:9); a reference, perhaps, to events which could not safely be written down. Epaphras, himself a Colossian, is at present with Paul (4:12). The presence of Luke (4:14) is not, as sometimes suggested, a problem.[1] Acts 19, granted, gives no sign of his presence in Ephesus with Paul (*i.e.* it is not a passage in which the writer says 'we' in referring to the movements of Paul and his companions). But (a) if Paul was in Ephesus for three years it is perfectly possible that Luke was with him for some, though not all, of that time, arriving and departing at different moments to the apostle; (b) even if Luke was there, and even if he did write Acts,[2] he was under no compulsion to record every imprisonment Paul suffered, and may well in fact have omitted to mention several which were of comparative insignificance. He tends only to record those from which some lessons can be learnt (*e.g.* Acts 16:16–40).

An extra argument for the Ephesian origin of Colossians, not usually noticed, is the close similarity we have already noted between our letter and 2 Corinthians, written (for the most part, at any rate) while Paul was on his way from Ephesus to Corinth, and referring to the sufferings Paul had undergone during his stay in Asia (2 Cor. 1:8). If we were to date Galatians during this same period,[3] the similarities between that letter and Colossians would also be of interest.

I am therefore inclined to put Colossians (and its com-

---

pp.43–45. See also Stuhlmacher, pp.21 f.; Houlden, p.139; Lohse, pp.165–167, 188; H. Koester, *Introduction to the New Testament*, vol.2, pp.130 ff.

[1] See Schweizer, p.26.

[2] See now the restatement of the case for Lucan authorship of Acts in I. H. Marshall, *The Acts of the Apostles: An Introduction and Commentary* (IVP/Eerdmans, 1980), pp.44–46. Compare M. Hengel, *Acts and the History of Earliest Christianity*, Eng. Tr. (SCM Press, 1979), pp.66 ff. and *idem, Between Jesus and Paul* (SCM Press, 1983), pp.97–128.

[3] Galatians has been dated both in the late 40s and in the middle 50s: see the discussion in J. A. T. Robinson, *Redating the New Testament*, pp.55–57. Schweizer (pp.127 f.), noting the parallels between Colossians and Galatians, argues from them that Galatians is aimed, as he thinks Colossians is, not at Judaism or Jewish Christianity but at some sort of syncretism. This seems to me exactly the wrong way round.

panion piece, Philemon) in the period between 52 and 55 (or possibly 53 and 56), while Paul was working in Ephesus (Acts 19:8–10).[1] It should be emphasized, however, that this, like all theories about the location of the captivity epistles, is simply a hypothesis. All that is claimed is that this particular hypothesis makes sense of the various bits of data involved; that it does so within a simple framework; and that it helps to explain certain features of the evidence in a particularly helpful way. Its especial significance for our understanding of Colossians is that it highlights the message of the letter as instruction given to a very young church.

If this solution is correct, we should be in a position to see its effect on the relationship between Colossians and Paul's other letters. We have suggested already that the similarities with 2 Corinthians are so striking as to constitute an extra argument for this dating, and that questions of theological differences with Romans and Galatians are not as weighty as is sometimes imagined. But the relationship between Colossians and Ephesians is obviously a special case. To read the two letters side by side is to be struck over and over again by close similarities of argument and wording, even though Ephesians lacks the Christological poem and the attack on false teaching which form the main features of Colossians.

This evidence poses a problem which is, fortunately, more tricky for students of Ephesians than for students of Colossians. By common consent, the two letters can be regarded as, in some senses, a rough draft and a fair copy of similar material. (In some senses, but not in all: Colossians is a perfectly good letter as it stands, highlighting different ideas; but where they overlap Ephesians looks the more polished.) Four main explanations of this phenomenon have received scholarly support:

i. Paul wrote Colossians first and then, perhaps soon afterwards, wrote Ephesians;
ii. Paul wrote Ephesians first, and then used some of the same material, in a different context, in writing Colossians;

[1]See Robinson, *ibid.*, pp.46 f., and compare G. B. Caird, *The Apostolic Age* (Duckworth, 1955), p.209.

iii. Paul wrote Colossians, and then an interpreter or friend used it as the basis for 'Ephesians', writing it as if it came from Paul;

iv. Paul wrote neither Ephesians nor Colossians, the latter being by an imitator of Paul and the former by an imitator of Colossians.

I have already argued that the fourth solution is unlikely. If we understand Paul's overall theology aright, Colossians falls comfortably within it. In addition, the idea that Ephesians, that majestic and noble work of art, is a copy of a copy ought to be regarded as the *reductio ad absurdum* of the theory. The third alternative is logically quite possible, and not particularly improbable in terms simply of literary style and content. It is quite conceivable that an early admirer of Paul would attempt to think his thoughts after him, drawing them together into a well-rounded whole: but, as we saw earlier, there is no reason to suppose that keeping company with a great writer produces of itself literary genius. Nor is it as easy as is often assumed to reconcile the exalted tone and material of Ephesians with the idea that the personal details of chapter 3, and of 6:19–22, are mere attempts at verisimilitude. And, as regards theology, the enlargement of Pauline horizons I have suggested, to show how Colossians coheres with Romans or Galatians, will comfortably take in Ephesians as well.

The choice between the first two solutions will depend on how we envisage Paul's mind at work in two different situations. It is not necessarily helpful to think only in terms of 'first draft' and 'final draft'; Paul was writing letters, not a doctoral dissertation. It is quite conceivable that somebody should pen an exalted piece of prose or even poetry and then, not long afterwards, write a letter into which a good deal of the earlier material would find its way, almost subconsciously, while more specific issues were being handled in a less formal style. It is misleading, also, though extremely popular, to think of Paul as working out his ideas from scratch while in the act of dictating. It is more likely by far that themes long mulled over are merely receiving fresh expression.

There is one argument which could tip the scales in favour of the chronological priority of Colossians. It appears from some very early manuscripts that the letter we call 'Ephesians' may not, originally, have borne an address.[1] The letter might, in that case, have been intended as a 'circular'. Even if the longer reading (including the address to Ephesus) is original, the manuscript variation shows at least that the letter was very early employed in this fashion, perhaps because it was believed that Paul had here deliberately drawn together the threads of his other writings, Colossians included. If the hypothesis of an Ephesian imprisonment fits Colossians, it is not inconceivable that Ephesians might have been a circular written, around the same time, to the church in Ephesus as it waited for his release, and also to the various churches which, like those in Colosse and Laodicea, had been planted in the neighbouring areas.[2]

Whichever letter came first, there is no evidence of a modification of ideas or a change in theology. Rather, parallel passages in the two letters may justifiably be used for mutual illumination. In none of his letters – not even Romans – does Paul attempt a full-dress presentation of 'everything he believes'. He draws out of his well-stocked repertoire of exegesis and theology only what he needs for each occasion. We may understand him better if, instead of playing off different writings against each other, we allow them to interact and interlock. And that, I believe, is achieved if we locate Paul in Ephesus, in the early 50s, while he is writing Colossians.

V. THE MESSAGE OF COLOSSIANS – THEN AND NOW

I have suggested that in Colossians Paul is drawing upon his overall theological understanding to help his readers find that genuine human and spiritual maturity which God wills for his people. God has done what the law, and 'Wisdom', could not do: sending his own Son in the likeness of sinful flesh, to

[1]See Metzger, *Textual Commentary*, p.601.
[2]This means that we do not have to accept the argument of Robinson, *Redating the New Testament*, p.64, that Ephesians, if authentic, rules out an Ephesian imprisonment as the place of origin for itself, and by implication for Colossians. For the possibility that Ephesians is the 'letter from Laodicea' of Col. 4:16, see the commentary on that verse.

achieve reconciliation, he dealt with sin on the cross, so that the life which the law had sought to give, the true life of God's people, might be brought to expression in those who, through faith and baptism, belong to Jesus Christ. The church need look – must look – nowhere else for forgiveness for the past, for maturity in the present, or for future hope. Faced with a young church in a small town in up-country Asia Minor, Paul has written a letter in which he has distilled his understanding of some of the greatest themes in theology.

But what may this all mean for the church at the end of the twentieth century? There are few, if any, Christians in the Lycus valley today. True, there are plenty of young churches elsewhere in the world, in need of growth to Christian maturity, but few if any of them will need Paul's warnings against the blandishments of Judaism. Again, by no means all modern Christians were practising members of a pagan religion before their conversion (though some were; and it is possible to view modern Western materialism as a sort of paganism, even if a rather boring one). These quite obvious points indicate that there is a gap, a distance, between our modern situation and that of the Colossians, and we should not lightly brush it aside. Nor can we casually solve the problem by elevating Paul's words into 'timeless truths', or by postulating such entities on the basis of what he says. One of the dangers with that approach is that it divides Scripture up into two sorts of material – that which is timeless, and that which is 'culturally conditioned'. In fact, *all* writing, including the Bible from Genesis to Revelation, is totally 'culturally conditioned'. It is only *within* the local, historically and culturally conditioned message of Paul to Colosse that later generations, ourselves included, may hear what the Spirit is saying to the church.

The Spirit and the church: there lie the clues which can help us to understand how we get from the ancient text to the modern situation. Paul intended his letters to be read out in church (4:16), and this reminds us that we cannot understand them in a purely individualistic setting. Each mature Christian has, of course, the responsibility to 'test all things'. But Christian truth is a *corporate* possession. The church is the context within which we should expect to have wrong ideas gently corrected and right ones gently suggested, and where we in turn may contribute to the same activities. This will mean active membership in a local church and perhaps a variety of Christian groups; it should also involve careful listening to Christians of other backgrounds and periods of history.

To set biblical interpretation within the context of the church, however, makes sense only if we hold a clear belief in the Spirit who enables the church to *be* the church. To hear Paul's words as if addressed to ourselves, we must understand ourselves both as parts of the same Spirit-filled community that he was addressing and as being ourselves indwelt by the Spirit who enabled Paul to write what he did. This will not solve all our problems of understanding or interpretation at a stroke. It will set them in the context where they can be worked at with faith and hope and (especially between disagreeing parties) love. It is part of God's plan for his people that they should wrestle, in reading the Bible, with puzzles and problems that a library of mere timeless truths would never produce, and thus to grow into a maturity appropriate for fully human beings.

We cannot, therefore, treat Colossians as merely a handbook of systematic theology. Systematic theology is a vital discipline, but reading the New Testament is not the same discipline. We cannot merely take Paul's composition apart and put its bits into other compositions of our own. We must listen to him in his own terms. That is when we will hear not only what he intended but also, perhaps, unexpected overtones and echoes which fit our own context. We must therefore make two journeys: the historian's journey, getting back to the original meaning, and the theologian's or preacher's journey, returning to our own time and place charged with the responsibility, under God, of speaking to our contemporary church and world of what we have heard. Biblical commentaries (certainly those in the present series) aim mainly to tackle the first journey. Even this, however, cannot be done without some degree of sympathy for the subject-matter, and the process of dialogue with the text necessary to achieve this will result in some pointers, at least, towards contemporary application. The attempt to hear what Paul was saying to the church in Colosse may, then, help us to hear what the Spirit is saying to the church today.

These two tasks will almost certainly not be identical. Not every church will need to be warned against a religion that exalts angels or encourages pseudo-spiritual asceticism. (Both, in fact, are right out of fashion in many Christian circles today, though there are some areas where they, or other things like them, flourish.) It would be wrong, in any case, to see Colossians as a warning against a 'super-spiritual' religion, against the idea that one is already living in heaven and can therefore sit light to earthly responsibilities.[1] On the contrary, Paul is writing to assure the Colossians that they really are, even now, citizens of heaven. There is, no doubt, a danger of proud over-confidence for those who believe this. Paul wrote 1 Corinthians partly in order to avert such a threat. But there is equal danger in failing to realize and enjoy all that it means to belong to Christ, to thank God for it and to live in the appropriate manner. This is perhaps a danger to which Protestants, anxious lest they give the church too high a status, are particularly subject. That seems to be partly why Colossians, and especially Ephesians, have been regarded in some quarters as incompatible with 'Pauline' – by which is often meant 'Protestant' – thought. For Paul, the church is the Body of Christ, already seated with her Lord in the heavenly places, as well as being called to suffer and work and witness in the world. To realize that one is complete in Christ is sure proof against the dangers of immature Christianity – the constant search for spiritual novelties, the unnecessary anxieties and fears over status or requirements, the pride over small 'achievements' – which threaten Christians in the modern world no less than in the ancient world.

The application of the polemic in Colossians 2 presents a particular problem. Some Christians, no doubt, need to be warned that to step into Judaism, or to attempt to combine it with Christianity, is to step back from the new age into the old. Others must not assume that this warning against Judaism is aimed primarily at 'legalism' or 'ritualism'. The emphasis of

---

[1]My interpretation of Colossians, and of its message for today, thus differs quite drastically from that proposed by R. C. Lucas in his commentary. I believe he is correct in his analysis of certain 'super-spiritual' trends in contemporary Christianity, and in his argument that they accord more with the spirit of the age than with genuine Christian faith. But I do not think that this is what Paul is talking about in Colossians.

Paul's attack is against the adopting of a 'national' or racial religion in preference to faith in the one who is Lord of all. The closest modern parallel might well be the idea that Christians should encourage each nation or race to follow its own particular gods. This suggestion is related to the extremely important point that each race, or individual, should be *allowed* (by the state) to follow its, his or her own god or gods. But it makes quite a different point, which would be valid only if we were falsely to identify religion and the law of the land. The view in question often claims that the same god is revealed in all the different religions; but this is not Paul's position. Christ is not one deity (certainly not a 'Western' one, as is sometimes claimed) among many. He is supreme over all. Monotheism has always been a scandal, as Paul well knew when he confronted Corinthian polytheism with the claim 'for us there is but one God . . . one Lord' (1 Cor. 8:6). This is his great claim in Colossians, too. It stands over against all idolatry, modern or ancient, and all theological relativism.

Within the life of the church, then, the letter to the Colossians will always have an important part to play. We, too, need to become mature as Christians and as human beings. We need to grow in our knowledge of who God is, of what he has done for us in Jesus Christ, and of how we can express our gratitude in worship and life. We, too, need the warning that true maturity, whether Christian or human, is not to be had by any other road. We are not Colossians, but we are Christians. Therein lies the problem of hermeneutics, and its solution.

COLOSSIANS: ANALYSIS

I. OPENING GREETING (1:1–2)

II. INTRODUCTION OF PAUL AND HIS THEME (1:3 – 2:5)

A. THANKSGIVING (1:3–8)
B. PRAYER AND MEDITATION (1:9–23)
    i. Paul's prayer: the knowledge of God (1:9–12a)
    ii. Reasons for thanksgiving (1:12b–23)
        a. The new exodus (1:12b–14)
        b. Creation and new creation in Christ (1:15–20)
        c. New creation in Colosse (1:21–23)
C. PAUL'S MINISTRY AND HIS REASONS FOR WRITING (1:24 – 2:5)
    i. Paul's ministry in Christ (1:24–29)
    ii. Paul's ministry to the Colossians (2:1–5)

III. THE APPEAL FOR CHRISTIAN MATURITY (2:6 – 4:6)

A. INTRODUCTION: CONTINUE IN CHRIST (2:6–7)
B. LET NO-ONE EXCLUDE YOU (2:8–23)
    i. Already complete in Christ (2:8–15)
        a. Christ and his rivals (2:8–10)
        b. Already circumcised in Christ (2:11–12)
        c. Already free from the law's demands (2:13–15)
    ii. Therefore, do not submit to Jewish regulations (2:16–23)
        a. These things were mere preparations for Christ's new age (2:16–19)

b. *With Christ you died to this world and its regulations* (2:20–23)

C. INSTEAD, LIVE IN ACCORDANCE WITH THE NEW AGE (3:1 – 4:6)
  i. *Live in Christ, the risen Lord* (3:1–4)
  ii. *Knowledge and life renewed according to God's image* (3:5–11)
  iii. *Do all in the name of the Lord Jesus* (3:12–17)
  iv. *New life – at home* (3:18 – 4:1)
  v. *New life – in the world* (4:2–6)

IV. FINAL GREETINGS (4:7–18)

A. INTRODUCTION OF MESSENGERS (4:7–9)
B. GREETINGS FROM PAUL'S COMPANIONS (4:10–14)
C. GREETINGS TO CHRISTIANS IN THE COLOSSE AREA (4:15–17)
D. SIGNATURE OF THE APOSTLE (4:18)

COLOSSIANS: COMMENTARY

I. OPENING GREETING (1:1–2)

Letters today have the sender's name at the end. In Paul's day, it came at the beginning, and was followed by a greeting to the recipients. The form is 'Paul; to the church in Colosse; greeting'. But the apostle has, as usual, expanded traditional style to set, right away, the scene and tone for what he wishes to say.

1. *Paul* does not come before the Colossians simply as a private individual, but as *an apostle of Christ Jesus*. Unlike most of the other apostles, he had not been a follower of Jesus during his earthly ministry; but he had been appointed, through his own vision of the risen Lord, to an office which, like theirs, gave him a special authority not only in churches he had founded himself but even in those which, like that in Colosse, he had not. It is this God-given authority which undergirds the continuing use of his writings as authoritative Scripture in the church. The supporting claim, that this apostleship came about *by* (literally 'through') *the will of God*, is not merely an indication of the ultimate source of this authority, but a linking of Paul's task to the over-arching divine plan of salvation which, prepared in the Old Testament and brought to a climax in the life, death and resurrection of Jesus Christ, was now being put into effect through the world-wide mission in which Paul had been allotted a key initiating role (see below, on 1:23).

Timothy our brother is included in the greeting, here and in the opening verses of 2 Corinthians, Philippians, 1 and 2 Thessalonians and Philemon. Among the most prominent of Paul's partners, travelling companions and assistants, Timothy shared a close bond of affection and mutual understanding with Paul, which is of course reflected in the two letters addressed to him personally, as well as in, *e.g.,* 1 Corinthians 16:10–11; Philippians 2:19–23.

2. The letter is addressed *to the holy and faithful brothers in Christ at Colosse;* not that Paul is differentiating between them and other Christians who were not 'holy and faithful' ('brother' is a frequent New Testament term for 'fellow-Christian', reflecting the fact that the church understood itself from the start as a family), but he looks at the church, with all its imperfections, from God's point of view (compare 1 Cor. 1:4–9, in the light of the rest of that letter). 'Holy' could be an adjective, as in NIV; it could be a noun ('saints'), as in RSV ('the saints and faithful brethren'); but even if this were so it would be quite wrong to see two different groups here. The 'and' would be, as often, explanatory ('the saints, *i.e.* the faithful brethren'). Paul often refers to Christians as 'saints', indicating thereby not an advanced level of holiness but the fact of being, through faith and baptism (see below, on 2:12), set apart from the world for God. The terms belong to the church as a whole, seen as the true people of God, the 'real Israel'.[1] The word 'faithful' is probably not to be taken in the sense of 'having Christian faith' – one could have deduced that from the fact that Paul calls them 'brothers' – but in the sense of 'firmly committed', 'steadfast'. The two phrases 'in Christ' and 'in Colosse' ('at' in NIV translates the Greek *en,* 'in') are nicely balanced in the Greek, standing on either side of the central phrase 'holy and faithful brothers'. This encourages us to take 'in Christ' in a locative sense, *i.e.* neither merely as a synonym for 'Christian' nor in a sense of 'mystical absorption', but as referring to the Messiah, the anointed King, *in whom* the true people of God find their identity. To be described as 'in Christ' and 'in Colosse' is to be located with precision in the purposes of God, as a member both of his true people and of that particular earthly community where one is called to service and witness.

[1] Moule, p.45.

47

Paul is writing to the Colossians with one great desire – that they should grow into full Christian maturity. It is in that light that his greeting is to be understood: *grace and peace to you from God our Father*[1] (this is an adaptation of conventional greetings formulae). 'Grace' sees Christian life and growth as the free gift of God; 'peace', with the overtones of the Hebrew word *shālôm*, encompasses not merely personal 'peace' of mind and heart, but all the wider blessings of belonging to God's covenant family. The scene is set for a letter through which Paul intends, by his writing, to be a means of that grace, and so to bring about that rich and mature peace (see, *e.g.*, 3:15).

II. INTRODUCTION OF PAUL AND HIS THEME (1:3 – 2:5)

This long introduction is often split up into almost unrelated parts (with 1:15–20 in particular being disassociated from the rest). But it is in fact a complex whole, at the end of which Paul is ready to move in to the heart of the letter. In it all, Paul is really introducing himself, so that the young church will understand that his writing to them at this time is simply one outflowing of his total God-given ministry. He says, in effect, 'this is how I am *thanking God* for you' (1:3–8), 'this is how I am *praying* for you' (1:9–23) and 'this is what I am *doing* for you' (1:24 – 2:5). In introducing himself like this he lays foundations for the main thrust of the letter, the maturity in Christ into which he hopes the Colossians will grow. Theologically, these foundations look like this: he tells the church that he thanks God for founding it (1:3–8), that he wants them to thank God for his great plan of salvation (1:9–20) and to appreciate where they fit into it (1:21–23) as well as the role of his own ministry within it (1:24 – 2:5). The 'therefore' of 2:6 shows that he is at that point ready to build on this carefully-laid foundation, bringing together God's gospel, the Colossian situation and his own vocation.

The exhortation of 2:6 ('just as you received Christ Jesus as Lord, continue to live in him') is therefore much more than the

---

[1] Several MSS add 'and the Lord Jesus Christ', but this is almost certainly a later addition.

rather obvious piece of advice which, taken out of context, it might appear to be. We will know, in fact, that we have understood 1:3 – 2:5 correctly when we discover that it has prepared us to give 2:6 its full value. When Paul there mentions 'Christ', the word is no mere empty cipher: it is the Christ of 1:15–20, in whom is true maturity (1:28), who is himself 'the mystery of God' (2:2), God's eternal secret plan for creating and redeeming the world. This large view of Christ must be kept in mind throughout.

A. THANKSGIVING (1:3–8)

Paul is able to address the Colossians as 'brothers in Christ', and to hope with confidence for God's grace and peace to be given to them, because he knows that God has already been at work amongst them. His characteristic way of mentioning this is not simply to remark that he has heard of their conversion, but to tell them that he thanks God for it. His extended introductory thanksgivings and intercessions – or rather, introductory *descriptions of* thanksgivings and intercessions – are thus an important feature of many of his letters (this is particularly true of Colossians, where thanksgiving forms an important theme: see 1:12ff.; 2:7; 3:15, 16, 17; 4:2). They are not 'asides', devotional musings detached from the main emphasis of the letter. They form, quite deliberately, the logical basis for what is to come. They illustrate, in addition, the principle they state. What is worked for must first be prayed for. The source of all peace is grace.

The detailed structure of the thanksgiving in verses 3–8 highlights the same point in a more precise way. After the initial statement that he is in constant prayer for them (v.3), which is reiterated in v.9 when Paul tells them the content of these intercessions, he outlines what it is that he thanks God for when he remembers them (vv. 4–5) and how it is that these things have come about (vv. 6–8). The paragraph gives us a valuable insight into Paul's understanding of how God's grace operates. The gospel, seen almost as a personified force, is at work in the world through those commissioned to proclaim it; where its truth is recognized and its command obeyed, it bears fruit. In a world where many varied 'religious experiences' were on offer, Paul gives the Colossians the theological framework of understanding within which they will be able to make sense of what God has been doing in their lives. Without this framework, experience remains ambiguous and even potentially misleading.

3. Though NIV and RSV both take *always* with *we thank God*, it goes more naturally in the Greek with *when we pray for you*: Paul is continually praying about the church in Colosse, and whenever he does so he thanks God. It is likely that the word 'always' indicates regularity, not that such prayers occupied all Paul's waking hours; he does not pray haphazardly or only when the mood takes him, but keeps regular hours of prayer (probably morning, noon and evening), and the church in Colosse is always mentioned. In this discipline of thanksgiving and intercession he was simply continuing a practice ingrained since his childhood – though of course (he would say) filling that practice with new content.

By praying to the God of Abraham, Isaac and Jacob as *the Father of our Lord Jesus Christ*, he is indicating that subtle but far-reaching development in his belief about God which took place when, on the road to Damascus, he was confronted with the fact that the God he had worshipped all his life had vindicated as Christ (*i.e.* Messiah) the Jesus whom he, Paul, had regarded as an impostor. Though Judaism knew God as Father, the precise nature of his paternal love could not be conceived until it had been revealed in the cross of the Messiah. Nor could that cross be understood, conversely, until it became clear that it was the climax of the saving plan of the God of Israel, and that therefore this God had now exalted the crucified one and given him the title 'Lord' (Greek *kyrios*). The familiar composite title for Jesus ('our Lord . . . Christ') is not, then, merely a heaping up of honorific phrases, but a very precise statement of who Jesus is from God's, and the church's, point of view. For Paul this meant nothing less than a new vision of God himself, which naturally began, as here, to be reflected in the nature and content of his prayers.[1]

[1]Moule (pp.47 f.) has a fine note on the structure of NT prayers.

4. As in various other passages (1 Cor. 13:13; 1 Thes. 1:3; 5:8), Paul draws together the three virtues of faith, hope and love. These are the things in the Colossian church for which he thanks God, both because they are fine and lovely in themselves and because they are signs of that new life which is springing up in Colosse: signs of peace and hence evidences of grace. But, unlike 1 Corinthians 13:13 (but like the two references in 1 Thessalonians), the order is 'faith – love – hope'. The phrase is not a mere formula, thrown in for effect, but a genuine statement in which each word counts. Each quality has its part to play in the development of the letter's thought (for faith, see 1:23; 2:7; for love, 1:8, 13; 2:2; 3:14; for hope, 1:23, 27).

Each is now further described. *Faith* is not just (as often today) any religious belief. It is defined as faith *in Christ Jesus*. This phrase (which could have the connotation of the sphere in which faith operates rather than, as an English reader tends to assume, the object of faith) is one of Paul's regular shorthand ways of describing characteristically Christian faith.[1]

Faith, for Paul, includes not only personal trust and commitment, but also the belief that certain things are true (see, *e.g.*, Rom. 10:9). These are brought together in, for instance, Romans 4:24 (belief *in* the God *who* raised Jesus). The present context emphasizes the truth of the gospel as something to be heard and acknowledged with the mind (vv. 5–6), and so stresses if anything the 'belief' side, though by no means at the expense of 'commitment'. 'Belief', if genuine, is more than just mental assent to truths.

For Paul, the sure sign of grace at work was the fact of a loving community created out of nothing: of a *love* not restricted to those with whom one has a natural affinity, but which extends to *all the saints*. It is this – perhaps after all in keeping with 1 Corinthians 13 – which Paul singles out in verse 8 as the main element in the news brought to him by Epaphras.

5. *Hope* here apparently refers not so much to the state or activity of hoping as to the thing hoped for. It is *the hope that is stored up for you in heaven* (*cf.* 1 Pet. 1:4, and especially 2 Tim.

---

[1] For alternatives, see, *e.g.*, Rom. 3:22, 26; Gal. 2:16; *etc.*

4:8). But how is the 'hope' connected to the previous verse? RSV ('because of the hope') preserves the ambiguity of the original, while NIV has attempted to clarify it by paraphrasing: 'the faith and love *that spring from* the hope . . .'. If this is correct – as grammatically it may be – it is an interesting and unusual idea. Paul normally sees faith and love, and hope, as together springing from the gospel, the facts about Jesus Christ. But the further references in 1:23, 27 may indeed suggest that Christian hope had formed a central part of Epaphras' initial preaching in Colosse. This element in Christianity would be quite new, and very attractive, for a pagan of the first century. So NIV may well have caught Paul's underlying meaning. The solid facts about the future hope of Christians are a powerful motivation for constant faith and costly love in the present. Paul does not say here what precisely it is that Christians hope *for*: it is not completely clear whether he envisages a heavenly realm already in existence waiting to be enjoyed by believers, or whether he simply refers to God's intention, and promise, concerning the bliss which he will give to his people. Galatians 4:26, however, encourages us towards the former view.

Paul uses the mention of hope as a bridge from the description of Christian existence in verses 4–5a to the description – still within the overall thanksgiving – of how this new life came about. The 'hope' is that which *you have already*[1] *heard about in the word of truth, the gospel*. 'The gospel', for Paul, is an announcement, a proclamation, whose importance lies in the truth of its content. It is not, primarily, either an invitation or a technique for changing people's lives. It is a command to be obeyed[2] and a power let loose in the world (*cf.* Rom. 1:16–17), which cannot be reduced to terms of the persuasiveness or even the conviction of the messenger. It works of itself to overthrow falsehood. It is, of course, quite likely that Paul has in mind a contrast with the false claims he opposes in chapter 2.

6. As Paul looks at the young church, what he sees is what

[1] Or 'before', as RSV. Those who think that false teachers had recently arrived in Colosse sometimes suggest that this refers to the time before their coming.

[2] *Cf.* Rom. 1:5; 6:16; 10:16; 15:18; 16:19; 2 Cor. 10:5; 2 Thes. 1:8; and see Lohse, p.21, esp. notes 71, 74.

God is doing: for, in personifying 'the gospel', he is really using a paraphrase to refer to the divine action *through* the gospel (and, of course, through its proclaimers, as in v.7). The gospel *has come to you*: God has reached out to them, has visited them with his saving power, as indeed *all over the world this gospel is producing fruit and growing*. Paul does not, of course, mean that every square mile of the inhabited earth has been evangelized (see below, on 1:23). From his perspective as a converted Pharisee the important point was that the salvation promised in the Old Testament had now been unleashed upon the world irrespective of geographical or racial barriers. His own missionary activity was an embodiment of this truth, as Ephesians 2:11 – 3:13 indicates. It is in that sense that the individual churches are 'representatives' of the gentile world as a whole. They were for Paul a sign and promise of the universal scope of God's saving purposes and hence of still greater things to come.

The gospel, treated metaphorically as a person at the start of verse 6, now becomes a plant which, like the good seed in the parable, bears fruit and grows.[1] This is one of those points where, in the light of the chapter as a whole (see below, on 1:10 and 1:15ff.), we may be permitted to hear overtones or echoes from an important Old Testament passage. In Genesis 1, the initial statement of the creation of the world by the God of Israel, the command is given to the animal kingdom that it should 'be fruitful and increase in number' (1:22). This is repeated (1:28) to the man and the woman who have just been created in the image and likeness of God. This theme from the creation account is picked up at several key points in the story of the creation of Israel, the family of Abraham, highlighting the Jewish belief that in the call of Israel God was fulfilling his purposes for the whole world, undoing the sin of Adam by creating for himself a holy people.[2] It is completely in line with Paul's rethinking of Jewish belief in the light of the gospel that he should transfer to that gospel ideas belonging to the creation, and the divinely intended recreation, of the world. Paul gives us an advance glimpse of the theological position soon to be stated

---

[1] Mk. 4:8 and parallels. Paul's image here, however, is not of cereal crops but of a tree.
[2] *Cf.* (with Gn. 1:26ff.) Gn. 17:2, 6, 16, 20; 22:17; 26:4, 24; 28:3; 35:11; *etc.*, as well as Gn. 8:17; 9:1, 7; Je. 3:16; 23:3.

in full (1:15–20). God is doing through the gospel what he always intended to do. He is sowing good seed in the world, and preparing to reap a harvest of human lives recreated to reflect his glory.

This, Paul now affirms, is no abstract theory. The gospel has been at work all over the world, *just as it has been doing among you*, in Colosse itself. Without wishing to press the plural form of 'you' (Greek *en hymin*) too far, it seems clear from verse 4 and elsewhere that Paul does not merely mean that 'among them' there is evidence of individual changed lives; he sees that 'in them' as a community the gospel has been at work to create that corporate life and love which is God's will for his family. In an individualistic age we do well to remind ourselves how often Paul's 'you' is plural – and that not merely referring to a collection of individuals, but indicating a corporate unity, the Body of Christ.

The gospel has been at work in Colosse *since the day you heard it and understood God's grace[1] in all its truth* (the words 'all its' in NIV are an explanatory gloss; RSV is closer to the original with 'the grace of God in truth'). God does not put his saving power into operation by some automatic or magic process which bypasses the consciousness of its recipients. Paul describes the effect of Epaphras' preaching in Colosse in terms not of an emotional reaction, nor even of people 'accepting Christ into their hearts', but of hearing truth and understanding it. The task of the apostolic herald is to announce truth: the word here translated 'understood' indicates that the response sought is an intelligent thinking through and recognition of that truth. Paul was in no doubt about the Colossians' state of heart, but he knew that Christian emotion must be undergirded with a clear-headed grasp of truth. It is important to stress at the same time that the response to the gospel will involve not only the intellect but also the emotions; but it should also be said that intellect and emotions, head and heart, are not simply two separate compartments without an adjoining door. Clear recognition and understanding of the genuine Christian gospel – that God loved

[1]For the use of 'grace' as a summary of the gospel events and their significance, *cf.* 2 Cor. 8:9.

the world so much that he gave his Son to die for it – is a most powerful stimulus to full-hearted Christian love for God in return. Such an emotional response can in its turn fuel the desire for a deeper intellectual understanding (see 1:9) of God's nature and purposes.

7–8. Part of the mystery of that work of grace is that it includes the proclamation itself. *You learned it from Epaphras* (as in the RSV, so in the Greek, this is still part of the same sentence). God's grace characteristically operates through the divinely appointed means (see Rom. 10:14–15). This is certainly not to set bounds to the sovereign grace of God. It is to note that, as a normal 'rule', God has committed himself to working through the proclamation of the gospel. The divine action takes up within itself both the work of the evangelist and the understanding of the hearers. When God works, humanity is not obliterated or bypassed but, through submission to the cross and all that it implies for preacher and hearer, it is enhanced, ennobled, redeemed. Epaphras does whole-heartedly the work to which he is called, as Paul's *dear fellow-servant*, working for Christ alongside him not in competition but in love, and thus being *a faithful minister of Christ on our behalf*, doing in Colosse what Paul himself would have done. Indeed, he is in some sense carrying out Paul's own work, by sharing in his unique mission to the Gentiles. This phrase also acts as a gentle indication of his (Paul's) own right to address them: they are Epaphras' work, but Epaphras is working on his, Paul's, behalf. (Some manuscripts read 'on your behalf'; even if this were correct,[1] Paul would still be linking Epaphras' work to his own by means of the adjective 'faithful', *i.e.* 'trustworthy'.) And as Epaphras works, God works; as he preaches, God opens the understanding of the hearers; as he lays before them the facts about Jesus, they recognize those facts as true. Like a man who suddenly learns that he has inherited a fortune, the Colossians are possessed of new knowledge which cannot but revolutionize their lives.

That this miracle has happened in Colosse, and that it is

[1] See Metzger, pp.619 f.; Lohse, p.23, n.90.

indeed nothing other than the work of God, is what Paul has now learnt on Epaphras' return: he has *also told us of your love in the Spirit*. No mere human affection, this: it is a love which, created by the Spirit (here mentioned explicitly for the first time, though the entire paragraph is incomprehensible without him), is God's own love, becoming their own through the miracle of grace, enabling them to give to one another that love which can be recognized by its likeness to God's own act of love on Calvary (see Rom. 5:5–10; *etc.*).

When we stand back from this opening paragraph, we see that, though in one sense it is about the Colossian church, in another sense it is about God. Already in his opening thanksgiving Paul has begun to reveal the truth he most wishes the Colossians to grasp: that in Christ God is the creator and re-creator of the world and of humanity, and that therefore, once the meaning of the cross is fully understood, the world and humanity are to be joyfully affirmed as his own. In Christ there is a new beginning, a new Genesis.

B. PRAYER AND MEDITATION (1:9–23)

These verses form a single unit, which is essentially a reported prayer. The reason why this is often overlooked is because most of the material, namely verses 13–23, is built on the final main element in the prayer, *i.e.* thanksgiving. Paul prays that the young church will grow in knowledge (v.9), in holiness (v.10) and in spiritual power (v.11), adding a few phrases to fill out the petition in each instance; then, finally, he prays that they will continually give thanks to God (v.12), this time filling out the meaning not with a few phrases but with several sentences. They are to thank the God *who* . . .: their knowledge of God and their thanksgiving to him is to be Christ-shaped.

i. Paul's prayer: the knowledge of God (1:9–12a)

The link with the opening thanksgiving (*for this reason*) should not be overlooked. It is because of what God has already done that Paul can pray with confidence for what God *will* do. Having begun a work of grace, God will continue and complete it (see Phil. 1:6). And this prayer is tireless: *we have not stopped praying for you* (see above, on 1:3) *since the day we heard about you*. In an echo of verse 6, Paul stresses that his response to Epaphras' news was just as immediate as their response to his preaching. The 'we' may include Timothy, but it could be simply rhetorical.

Paul's habit of reporting his regular prayers on behalf of his addressees (see, *e.g.*, Rom. 1:9ff.; Phil. 1:9; *etc.*) should not go unremarked. He will not offer teaching, advice and encouragement except in the context of prayer. His apostolic work is not his own idea. It is part of God's plan. Conversely, prayer brings the assurance that his ministry is being used within God's overall plan (1:24–29), and consequently that characteristic confidence which, outside this context, could sound like arrogance.

9. Basic to the whole prayer is the opening phrase: *asking God to fill you with the knowledge of his will* (in the Greek the verb 'fill' is passive, 'that you may be filled'; NIV has made explicit the regular use of the passive to refer obliquely to the divine action). It is this 'knowledge' which forms the basis both of holiness (v. 10) and of thanksgiving (vv. 12ff., in the light of 2:2), and which is the central characteristic of the humanity that is now renewed in Christ (3:10). The 'knowledge of God's will' is more than simply an insight into how God wants his people to behave: it is an understanding of God's whole saving purpose in Christ, and hence (as in v. 10b) a knowledge of God himself. Some have seen in the word 'knowledge' *(epignōsis)* a hint that Paul is picking up the language (and, by implication, refuting the teaching) of 'gnostic' opponents – religious groups which, drawing on many traditions, held out the offer of a salvation attained through spiritual 'knowledge' *(gnōsis)*, which would enable one to escape from the material world and realize one's true ('spiritual') destiny. There is, however, no evidence of such teaching in any clearly defined form at this period, and when it does appear it is probably itself dependent on Christianity.

What Paul is speaking of here is not an esoteric knowledge, confined to private religious experience or exclusive sects. It is a knowledge 'of his (*i.e.* God's) will', which is open to all God's people. This knowledge is given *through all spiritual wisdom and understanding*. RSV's 'in' is a more literal rendering than NIV's 'through': knowledge of God's will *manifests itself in* these qualities. The two adjectives ('all' and 'spiritual') govern both the nouns ('wisdom' and 'understanding'). Their regular secular meaning ('wisdom' is mental excellence in general, 'understanding' is the ability to think through a subject coherently and clearly) is thus transposed on to a plane of more than merely human or worldly intellectual skill.

The three terms 'knowledge', 'wisdom' and 'understanding', so important elsewhere in Paul, are therefore best understood against their Old Testament and Jewish background, in which they regularly denote aspects of that character which God seeks to inculcate in his people.[1] 'Wisdom' is the characteristic of the truly human person, who takes the humble yet confident place marked out for Adam in the order of creation, under God and over the world. For Christians to 'grow up' in every way will include the awakening of intellectual powers, the ability to think coherently and practically about God and his purposes for his people. Paul never plays off spiritual life against intellectual understanding. The wisdom and understanding commended here are given the adjective 'spiritual', and at once expounded in practical and ethical terms in verse 10.

10. Verses 9 and 10, taken together, form a miniature picture of Christian life and growth. The argument is not circular (as might at first appear), but spiral. Paul prays that they may increase in knowledge of God's will, with the result that the Colossians will live as God wants them to and so increase in the knowledge of God! Understanding will fuel holiness; holiness will deepen understanding. (An alternative, which I consider less likely, is that the phrase at the end of v.10 means 'by means of the knowledge of God'.) When Paul says *that you may lead a life* (NIV adds, in front of those words, *and we pray this in order*, to make the thought clear) he uses the verb 'to walk', in keeping

---

[1] See, *e.g.*, Ex. 31:3; 35:31, 35; Dt. 34:9; Is. 29:14; *etc.*; and, from Qumran, 1QS 4:4, 1QSb 5:25, 1QH 12:11ff. (Vermes, pp.76, 209, 189); and other refs. in Lohse, pp.25 f. See too Rom. 2:18.

with his Jewish background (*cf.*, in the Old Testament, Pr. 2:20; 4:25–27; *etc.*). This 'walk' must be *worthy of the Lord*. The Lord, Jesus Christ, provides in his death and resurrection a pattern of life which sets the standard for his people. Those who are 'in the Lord' must live appropriately. The following clause, '(that you) *may please him in every way*', is not expressing an impossible ideal. Paul knows that complete perfection is attained only with the eventual gift of the resurrection body (Phil. 3:12). Nevertheless, those who belong to Christ can and do please God (*cf.* Rom. 12:1–2; 2 Cor. 5:8, 1 Thes. 4:1). God looks on his new (albeit as yet incomplete) creation, and declares it to be very good.

This explanation is supported by another oblique allusion to Genesis 1. Just as the gospel is bearing fruit and growing, so God's people are themselves *bearing fruit in every good work*, and *growing in the knowledge of God* (the Greek verbs are the same as those in v.6). Here is the typically Pauline paradox of grace. God is at work, *therefore* his people are at work (see further, on 1:29). This (albeit indirect) reference to Genesis increases the awareness that what Paul is talking about is God's new creation. He is asking that the Colossians may understand themselves more and more to be God's new, true humanity, and that they may increasingly live in a manner appropriate to that vocation. The idea of 'good works' is of course thoroughly Pauline (see Rom. 13:3; 2 Cor. 9:8; Gal. 6:10; Tit. 1:16, and the parallel to our present passage in Eph. 2:10). By adding 'in every good work' to 'bearing fruit' and 'in the knowledge of God' to 'growing' he has expanded the formula of verse 6, neatly integrating what we often see as the active and reflective aspects of Christian living. Knowing God is itself an activity; obeying him is a form of devotion.

11–12a. The remainder of the prayer indicates the power which enables the young church to grow in this way and the thankful attitude which will characterize them as they do so (RSV weakens this close connection with vv.9–10 by beginning a new sentence here). God is accomplishing this productive and growing Christian character in his people so that they are *strengthened with all power according to his glorious might*. God is regularly seen in the Old Testament as the powerful God – the sovereign creator who rescued Israel from Egypt. That power, unleashed through the gospel (see Rom. 1:16–17; 1 Cor. 1:24; *etc.*), is now continually at work in God's people to give them *great endurance and patience*.[1] Paul singles out these qualities as the weapons one needs to live in the world undaunted by its crises and panics. A patient and longsuffering spirit, the quiet corollary of faith, hope and love, is the product of the settled conviction that the Father of Jesus Christ is the sovereign Lord of the world, and that he is able to bring about his purposes in his own time and manner. There is a slight distinction to be drawn between 'endurance' and 'patience'. The former is what faith, hope and love bring to an apparently impossible situation, the latter what they show to an apparently impossible person. Verse 11 contributes to the total prayer the insights (a) that growth in the knowledge of God, and in holiness, is an uphill battle, and (b) that strength for this battle can only come – but will surely come – from the power of God himself.

Since the early manuscripts of the New Testament contain almost no punctuation, it is impossible to tell whether *joyfully* goes with *giving thanks* in verse 12 (as NIV) or with 'endurance and patience' in verse 11 (as RSV). But, as verse 12 is a continuation of the same sentence, it makes little overall difference. God's strength equips his people to live in the world with patience and to praise him for his grace. These thanks are to be offered *to the Father*. Christian maturity stems from a proper, thankful relationship to God, not as a remote or unconcerned being, but as the wise and loving Father of his people.

ii. *The reasons for thanksgiving* (1:12b–23)

a. The new exodus (1:12b–14). Paul is not content merely to tell his readers to be thankful. He gives them three good reasons for gratitude. These (vv. 12–14, 15–20, 21–23) are not just stated side by side, but depend closely upon each other. Genuine Christian theology is the exploration of God's character and actions, not in a spirit of mere speculation and curiosity, but

[1] *Cf.* Is. 40:28–31.

out of gratitude and love, and with the intention of, and desire for, obedience. Paul's prayer for the church reaches its climax in thanksgiving, and this thanksgiving is to be based on knowledge.

12b. The first reason for thanksgiving is that the Colossians have been given a share in the new exodus, the deliverance of the true people of God – the God, that is, *who has qualified you*[1] *to share in the inheritance of the saints in the kingdom of light.* This seems at first sight a complicated way of saying that God has caused the Colossians to hear and receive the gospel. That is indeed Paul's underlying meaning. But expressing it thus enables Paul to evoke a whole world of imagery relating to Israel's exodus from Egypt and her entry into the promised land. The 'inheritance' alludes to the promised land of Canaan; 'the saints' is a regular term for the people of God, indicating that they are set apart from the world for his service.[2] The parallel in Ephesians 2:11–13 suggests the idea that the heritage of God's people is no longer the prerogative of one race, but has been opened up so that people of every conceivable background can share it. The promise of the land is widened into the promise of a whole new creation (Rom. 4:13; 8:17–25). The addition of 'in light' differentiates between the new and the old inheritance (the glory of heaven, not the land of Canaan) and also sharpens the moral contrast with the kingdom of darkness (v.13), where the young Christians had formerly dwelt.

The Colossians have not come into this inheritance automatically. God has 'made them fit' for it. Paul elsewhere uses this word (in Greek *hikanōsanti*) and its cognates when describing a status or office for which he was not 'fit' in himself, but for which God 'fitted' him (see, *e.g.,* 1 Cor. 15:9; 2 Cor. 2:16; 3:5–6). He now explains this divine action further, in order the

---

[1] Two good MSS read 'you'; and, though the great majority of MSS have 'us', this is probably caused by assimilation to 'us' in the following verse.

[2] This apparently natural understanding of 'saints' has been challenged by some recent writers who, on the basis of impressive parallels from Qumran, take it to refer to angels (see Lohse, p.36). This seems to me to conflict with Paul's regular theology: God's people inherit not angelic privileges – that is, according to many scholars, one of the ideas Colossians is written to counteract – but precisely *human* ones. These, in the light of the incarnation, are if anything actually greater, not less, than those of the angels.

more securely to ground the Colossians' thanksgiving.

13. Again he alludes to the exodus, this time referring particularly to the dramatic rescue operation in which God delivered his people from the dark power of Egypt (see Ex. 6:6; 12:27; 14:30), transferring them into a new land: *for he has rescued us from the dominion of darkness and brought us into the kingdom of the Son he loves.* The harsh rule of the prince of darkness has been exchanged for the wise sovereignty of God's Son (*cf.* Rom. 5:21; 6:16ff.). Paul shares with other New Testament writers, and with Jesus himself, the belief in the existence of a dark power to whom the human race, and the world, is subject because of sin – and the belief that, in Jesus Christ, God has defeated this power and is establishing his own kingdom in its place.

On the basis of 1 Corinthians 15:23–28 we may infer – though the point is controversial – that Paul conceived of the establishment of this kingdom as a two-stage process. First there is 'the kingdom of Christ', which begins with Christ's resurrection and exaltation and continues until all enemies are subdued. Then there comes the final kingdom of God, the restoration of all things. This distinction does not, of course, correspond directly to the language about God's kingdom on the lips of Jesus; it belongs to a later perspective. The idea of the 'kingdom' is not found frequently in Paul (see Rom. 14:17; 1 Cor. 6:9), but is clearly presupposed throughout. The language of 1:13 is, in fact, firmly grounded in the world of Jewish expectations and in the fulfilment of those hopes in the Messiah, Jesus.

There are two closely related reasons why Paul has described Jesus as 'the Son he loves' (literally 'the Son of his love'; *cf.* RSV, 'his beloved Son'). There is, first, an allusion to Jesus' baptism,[1] when God anointed him with his Spirit, and said 'you are my Son, whom I love; with you I am well pleased' (Mk. 1:11), thus declaring Jesus to be the anointed King of Israel, the one in whom Israel's destiny is summed up and fulfilled. Hence, secondly, God has fulfilled 'in him' his ancient purposes. Jesus

---

[1]Jesus' baptism may have left other traces in Paul's writings, *e.g.* Rom. 1:3–4. Whether or not Col. 1:13–14 is itself a poetic reference to Christian baptism it is hard to say for certain. But the language would fit such a context (*cf.* 1 Cor. 10:1ff.) and Paul, building on this passage, develops ideas about baptism in 2:11ff.

as the beloved Son is Jesus as the true Israel. He has offered to God the filial obedience which Israel had not: 'when Israel was a child, I loved him, and out of Egypt I called my son' (Ho. 11:1, quoted of Jesus in Mt. 2:15). This exodus reference fits well with the rest of our present passage. In Christ the love of God has been expressed and defined by being lived out, by being put to death to redeem sinners.

14. *In him, then, we have redemption,*[1] *the forgiveness of sins.* The word 'redemption', as used in the ancient world in general, is from a root which carried the meaning (capable of metaphorical use) of 'purchase from the slave-market'. To a Jew, however, the root in question would always awaken deeper echoes, memories of the time when God redeemed his people from the kingdom of Pharaoh.[2] As a result the 'forgiveness of sins' here is not merely good news for troubled consciences, though of course it certainly is that. It is one of the specific blessings of the new covenant spoken of in Jeremiah 31:31ff. and Ezekiel 36:16-36.[3] This idea belongs within the wider Jewish belief that God's purposes for Israel were part of his plan to rid the world of evil entirely. It is this plan that he has now put into effect.

Paul, then, is asserting in shorthand form that in Christ, the true Israel, the true King, the one whom God loves, God's people are rescued from the dark power that has enslaved them and are brought into all the blessings of membership in the new covenant. Chief among these blessings is the fact that sin has been dealt with. God's people are to thank him that they are indeed his people, qualified for inheritance (v.12), delivered from sin's grim tyranny (v.13), redeemed through his Son (v.14). This statement (and its further application in vv. 21-23) must have considerably clarified for the young Christians in Colosse exactly what it was that had happened to them in their conversion, and why it had been necessary.

b. Creation and new creation in Christ (1:15-20). The next six

---

[1]Some MSS add 'through his blood', presumably because of the parallel with Eph. 1:7.
[2]See Caird, pp.171-174, and D. Hill, *Greek Words and Hebrew Meanings: Studies in the Semantics of Soteriological Terms* (CUP, 1967), pp.53 ff.
[3]See too, *e.g.*, 1QS 3:6-12; 11:2-5 (Vermes, pp.75, 92).

verses of the letter are generally, and rightly, reckoned among the most important Christological passages in the New Testament. It is perhaps inevitable, therefore, that they should have been the subject of considerable discussion. The present work is not the appropriate place to engage in these debates: what follows presupposes the results of detailed work set out elsewhere.[1]

1. *Poem and context*
Most scholars agree that the passage is skilfully worded and rythmically balanced, deserving to be called a poem. Some have gone beyond this, and suggested that it is, or contains, a hymn already well known before being quoted here. Many hypotheses as to the origin and original shape of this hymn have been suggested, but none has met with great support.[2] There are reasons, however, for questioning some aspects of this approach:

(a) Verse 15 begins with 'who is . . .', suggesting that the hymn does not begin there.

(b) Verses 12–14 are also in an elevated style.

(c) There is no need, as is sometimes supposed, to delete words or phrases to produce a credible poetic structure (see below).

(d) The poem as it stands fits very well into its present context, continuing and bringing to a climax the reasons why the Colossians should thank God.

(e) It also fits very well into the thought of the whole letter.

(f) If Paul has edited the hymn by adding bits, it is quite arbitrary to suppose he would not also have left bits out; if so, restoration of the 'original' is out of the question.

In short, if these verses ever had a meaning other than that which they now bear, we could never be sure that we knew it. The meaning they now have, *i.e.* the contribution they make to the larger unit within which they occur, is clear: and that is what we need when studying Colossians.

2. *Poetic structure*
The structure of the poem can be clearly seen by highlighting

---

[1] See my article, 'Poetry and Theology in Col. 1:15–20', forthcoming in *NTS*.
[2] See the summaries in O'Brien, pp.31 ff.; Schweizer, pp.55–63; Martin, pp.61–64.

the connecting words which introduce each line or group of lines. There are four sections. The outer two begin with 'who is . . .', the inner two with 'and he . . .'. The balance of the detailed content (even more impressive in the original; the English here is as literal as possible) shows that this is a helpful approach.

(Section 1)
15a   Who is the image
          of God, the invisible one
15b   firstborn of all creation
16a   for in him everything was created
16b   in the heavens and on the earth
16c   the visible and the invisible
                whether thrones or dominions
                whether rulers or authorities
16d   everything has been created
                through him and unto him.
(Section 2)
17a   and he is before all things
17b   and all things in him hold together
(Section 3)
18a   and he is the head
                of the body, the church[1]
(Section 4)
18b   Who is the beginning
18c   the firstborn from the dead
18d   so that in everything he might become pre-eminent
19   for in him all God's fullness
                was pleased to dwell
20a   and through him to reconcile
                everything to him(self)[2]
20b   making peace through the blood
                of his cross (through him)[3]
20c   whether things on the earth
                or things in the heavens.

[1]Sections 3 and 4 are much more clearly balanced in Greek than is possible in English.
[2]See the discussion in the commentary.
[3]These words are omitted from a good many MSS: see Metzger, p.621.

It should be clear from this that there are all sorts of parallels between the different parts of the poem. The first lines of sections 1 and 4 belong together: so do the opening lines of sections 2 and 3. The poem pivots about the division between verses 17 and 18. At a broader level, sections 1 and 4 both begin with a statement about Christ, amplify it with the title 'firstborn', and then explain it in relation to Christ's position *vis-à-vis* the created order. The sequence 'in him . . . through him . . . to him . . .' occurs in verse 16 and verses 19–20a. The symmetry of all these is not, of course, exact in all details, but there is no good reason to expect it to be.

3. *Poetic significance*

Someone who writes in this way wants his or her readers to stop and think. The most obvious point that the poem makes is the parallel between creation and new creation; hence the emphasis that is placed on the fact that each was accomplished by means of the same agent. The Lord through whom you are redeemed (Paul is telling the Colossians) is none other than the one through whom you (and all the world) were created.

This statement conforms closely to the basic confession of Judaism, that Israel's God is the creator God, and vice versa. (See, *e.g.*, Pss. 96:5; 146:5–6; Is. 40:12–31.) It is a typical statement of Jewish-style monotheism, and would be a telling rejoinder to any dualistic theology which saw creation as inherently bad.[1] But this form has been filled with new content. What was before said in reference to Israel's God, Yahweh, is now said in reference to Jesus Christ. He has not displaced the God of Abraham, the God of the exodus. He has made him known. If the hymn stands, with mainline Judaism, over against paganism, it also stands over against Judaism itself. We might compare 1 Corinthians 8:1–6, where Paul fills the Jewish confession ('the Lord our God is one Lord') with Christian content.

This point is undergirded by the particular language used of Jesus in the poem. As far back as 1925 C. F. Burney made the brilliant suggestion that the hymn deliberately applies to Jesus

---

[1] This means that the hymn, or any earlier form of it that might be imagined, has nothing whatever to do with either gnosticism proper (as Käsemann suggested: see Lohse, p.45, and p.60, n.205) or with a 'gnosticizing trend' (Martin, p.65).

everything that could be said of the figure 'Wisdom' by com-
bining Genesis 1:1 ('In the beginning God created', in Hebrew
berēshith . . .) with Proverbs 8:22, where 'Wisdom' states that
'the LORD begat me at the beginning (*rēshith*) of his work'.[1] The
significance of this can be grasped in two syllogisms:

1. (a) 'Wisdom' is God's agent in the creation and preservation
of the world.[2]
   (b) Humanity is designed to be God's vicegerent on earth
(Gn. 1:26–28; Ps. 8:6–8).
   (c) Therefore 'Wisdom' is the attribute needed by human
beings to equip them for this task.
2. (a) Israel was called to be God's true humanity.[3]
   (b) The Jewish Law (*Torah*) was the charter of Israel's life.
   (c) Therefore *Torah* is to be identified with Wisdom.[4]

Against this background of thought, Burney's theory results
in the following view of 1:15–20.

(a) The divine Wisdom has at last been fully embodied in a
human form, Jesus the Messiah, Israel's representative.

(b) God's purposes in the creation of the world, and for the
world's redemption, are fulfilled in him.

(c) The Lord to whom the young Christians have given their
allegiance is not one cult-figure among many, but is the one
through whom was made the entire universe, all mere cult-
figures included.

(d) Redemption is not thought of dualistically, as though the
created world were totally evil and salvation meant being rescued from it. Creation is God's work – Christ's work: though
spoilt by sin, it still belongs to God and God still has plans for it.

---

[1]C. F. Burney, 'Christ as the *Archē* of Creation', in *JTS* 27, 1925–6, pp. 160–177. Burney,
surprisingly, never linked his interpretation to the mention of Christ as the Image of God in
v.15, which sets the tone for a reference to Gn. 1 throughout – which, as already argued, is
likely from earlier oblique references in Colossians. For the translation 'begat me', and a full
discussion showing that Pr. 8:22 is related directly to Paul's use of the noun 'firstborn', see
Burney, pp.160–173.
[2]See Jb. 28:25–27; Pss. 104:24; 139:14; Pr. 3:19–20; Is. 28:23–29; Je. 10:12–13.
[3]See my article, 'Adam in Pauline Christology' in *SBL 1983 Seminar Papers*, ed. K. H.
Richards (Scholars' Press, 1983), pp.359–389, here at 361–365.
[4]See, *e.g.*, Wisdom of Solomon 6 – 10; Ecclus. 15:1; 24:1–12; *etc.*

Redemption is not an invasion from a different or hostile realm. The Lord of this world has come to claim his rightful possession.

If they grasp even the outline of this picture (the detail is complex, but the shape is simple), the Colossians, who had gratefully turned away from their pagan 'gods' in becoming Christians, will not be inclined to go back to them. Nor will they be tempted (this, as we shall see, is the main point of ch. 2) to look to Judaism for protection *against* the pagan 'principalities and powers'. Having Christ, God's true Wisdom, the Lord of the world, they possess all they need (*cf.* 1 Cor. 3:22–23). If *Christ* is God's Wisdom, his *Torah*, then all that Judaism believed to be true of herself, and of her *Torah*, all that she hoped for because of her monotheism and election, has been achieved in Jesus Christ. He (not the Law) is the Father's agent in the world. He (not an abstract divine 'Wisdom') is supreme over the nations and their 'gods'. For him, not for Israel, all things were created.[1] This is the fundamental emphasis of the poem within the letter as whole.

4. *Jesus and God*

Paul, then, does not in this poem abandon the Jewish doctrines of monotheism and election. He redefines them. But what, in that case, is he asserting about Jesus, in particular when he calls him 'the image of God' (v.15)? There has been considerable debate about this from the first Christian centuries up to the present, and the answer offered below is an attempt to hold together the strong points of the various parties in the debate.[2]

(a) The actual reference of verse 15 is clearly the man Jesus, who is now exalted. Paul uses the present tense ('is') to refer to him as having taken the place of world sovereignty marked out for humanity ('the image of God') from the beginning (*cf.* Eph. 1:20–23).

(b) The logic of the hymn (creation – new creation) indicates also a reference to the exalted Jesus as the Father's agent in creation. The one through whom the world was made has now become, as a human being, the one through whom the world is

---

[1] For the idea that the world was created for the sake of Israel see my article, 'Adam in Pauline Christology', pp.362–364.

[2] The argument is set out more fully in my article referred to on p.64, n.1. above.

ruled by the saving love of God. The poem refers to the exalted man, but identifies him with the pre-existent Lord.

(c) There is therefore no suggestion that Jesus pre-existed in human form: merely that it was utterly appropriate for him, as the pre-existent one, to become man. The language Paul uses to refer to him before his human conception and birth is often borrowed from his later human life, just as we say 'the Queen was born in 1926', not meaning that she was then already Queen, but that *the person we now know as Queen* was born that year. Thus 2 Corinthians 8:9, 'For you know the grace of our Lord Jesus Christ, that though he was rich, yet for your sakes he became poor': not that the pre-existent one was already Jesus, the Messiah, but that *the person we now know as Jesus, the Messiah,* is to be identified as God's pre-existent agent.

(d) Paul's Jewish background supplied him with the categories for this breath-taking idea, but (as usual) he reworked them. Some Jews regarded 'Wisdom' or the Mosaic Law as quasi-divine pre-existent entities, not thereby compromising monotheism but expressing, in a figure of speech, certain aspects of God's character. Paul, likewise remaining an emphatic monotheist, applies these themes to Jesus, and can actually state (v.19; 2:9) that all the divine fullness dwells in him. 'Jesus' and 'God' do not, though, mean the same thing: Paul regularly distinguishes God as 'Father' and Jesus as 'Son' or 'Lord'. But Jesus is not a second God. His death (v.20) is the achievement of God himself. Paul regarded Jesus as identical with one who was, and always had been, fully divine, and yet who could be distinguished in thought from the Father. The pre-existent Lord of the world becomes Lord of the church (1:18–20) in order to become Lord, fully, of the world which he has made but which has rebelled against him.

(e) The Colossians (this is the point of this theology in its context) have thus given their allegiance not to one cult-figure among others, but to the divine Lord through whom the world was made. The redemption achieved in Christ is indeed the new Genesis: the church really is the new humanity (3:10–11). The Jews learnt more fully who their God was when he redeemed them from Egypt (see Ex. 3:1–17; 6:1–8); the world may now learn through the gospel the full truth about the God who made it. The 'exodus' ideas of 1:12–14 thus belong exactly where they are in relation to the poem. The incarnation and crucifixion of Jesus were self-revealing, self-fulfilling actions which the one creator God was pleased to undertake (*cf.* 2 Cor. 5:19 with Col. 1:19–20). The poem leaves the church, and the world, not just with a picture of the exalted Christ, but with a vision of the gracious, loving and beckoning creator-redeemer God.

15. It remains to fill in the details of the poem, to show how this wealth of theology was actually expressed. *He*, the Son of God in whom we have redemption, *is the image of the invisible God*. No-one has ever seen God, wrote John in his Prologue (1:18), but God the only Son[1] has made him known. Humanity was made as the climax of the first creation (Gn. 1:26–27): the true humanity of Jesus is the climax of the history of creation, and at the same time the starting-point of the new creation. From all eternity Jesus had, in his very nature, been the 'image of God', reflecting perfectly the character and life of the Father. It was thus appropriate for him to be the 'image of God' as man: from all eternity he had held the same relation to the Father that humanity, from its creation, had been intended to bear. Humanity was designed to be the perfect vehicle for God's self-expression within his world, so that he could himself live appropriately among his people as one of themselves, could rule in love over creation as himself a creature. God made us for himself, as Augustine said with a different, though perhaps related, meaning. The doctrine of incarnation which flows from this cannot, by definition, squeeze either 'divinity' or 'humanity' out of shape. Indeed, it is only in Jesus Christ that we understand what 'divinity' and 'humanity' really mean: without him, we lapse into sub-Christian, or even pagan, categories of thought, and then wonder why the doctrine of incarnation causes us so much difficulty. Paul's way of express-ing the doctrine is to say, poetically, that the man Jesus fulfils the purposes which God had marked out *both* for himself *and* for

---

[1] So NIV, grasping the nettle presented by the diversity of variant readings: see Metzger, p.198, and Leon Morris, *The Gospel According to John* (Marshall, Morgan and Scott, 1972), pp.113 f.

humanity.[1]

Upon Jesus Christ, then, has come the role marked out for humanity, and hence for Israel: Christ is *the firstborn over all creation*. The title 'firstborn' is given to Israel in the Old Testament (Ex. 4:22; Je. 31:9; *cf*. Psalms of Solomon 18:4; 4 Ezra 6:58), and also, once, to the coming Davidic Messiah (Ps. 89:27). Burney (see above) argued strongly that it referred to the figure of Wisdom in Proverbs 8:22. It therefore conveys the idea of priority in both time and rank, and we should not foreclose on either of these options (NIV, in its paraphrase, allows only the idea of rank): to opt for temporal priority does not imply that the pre-existent Son of God is merely the first created being. The continuing temporal sense of the word is clear from verse 18 (*cf*. Rom. 8:29), and gives a parallel idea to that expressed in the NEB translation of John 1:1, 'When all things began, the Word already was'. It is *in virtue of* this eternal pre-existence that the Son of God holds supreme rank.

16. That this is the correct way to read verse 15 is immediately confirmed: *for by him all things were created*. He is not simply part of the created world itself. All that God made, he made by means of him. Paul actually says 'in him', and, though the word *en* can mean 'by' as well as 'in',[2] it is better to retain the literal translation than to paraphrase as NIV has done. Not only is there an intended parallel with verse 19, which would otherwise be lost: the passive 'were created' indicates, in a typically Jewish fashion, the activity of God the Father, working *in* the Son. To say 'by', here and at the end of verse 16, could imply, not that Christ is the Father's agent, but that he was alone responsible for creation.

All things, which in the Greek has an article indicating that Paul sees this created world as a single whole (*i.e.* 'the totality'), is now further specified: *things in heaven and on earth, visible and invisible, whether thrones or powers or rulers or authorities*. (NIV obscures the parallel between this verse and 2:15 by translating

---

[1]For the whole idea, see also 2 Cor. 4:4 in the context of 3:18; 4:6; 5:17–21; Rom. 8:29. There is an obvious link, also, with the idea of Christ as Last Adam: see Rom. 5:12–21; 1 Cor. 15:20–49; on which see my article, 'Adam in Pauline Christology'.

[2]Moule, p.65.

archai in 1:16 as 'rulers' and in 2:15 as 'powers'.) Wherever you look, or whatever realities you think of, you discover entities which, even if they do not acknowledge the fact, owe their very existence to Christ. They are his handiwork. Paul has here chosen to mention especially what we today call the power structures of the universe.

The identity of these 'powers' is much debated. Some of the terms Paul uses here belonged to complex metaphysical systems in contemporary non-Christian thought. It is not easy to separate the different terms clearly. 'Thrones' is probably superior to 'powers', 'rulers' to 'authorities'; and while 'thrones' and 'rulers', in the Greek, connote the position held, 'powers' and 'authorities' indicate the presence of those over whom authority is exercised. Paul, however, is not concerned so much with listing them in a particular order, or with distinguishing carefully between them, as with asserting Christ's supremacy over them. As to their referent, in our modern age it has often been taken for granted that Paul's language about supernatural power-structures needs to be demythologized, to be turned into language about (say) international power politics or economic 'structures'. This is quite legitimate, since for Paul spiritual and earthly rulers were not sharply distinguished.[1] In his view, earthly rulers held authority (in the sense intended by Jn. 19:11; Rom. 13:1–7) only as a trust from the creator.[2] At the same time, we should not ignore the supernatural or 'demonic' element in these 'powers'. Anything to which human beings offer the allegiance proper only to God is capable of assuming, and exerting, a sinister borrowed power.[3] For Paul, the 'powers' were unseen forces working in the world through pagan religion, astrology, or magic, or through the oppressive systems that enslaved or tyrannized human beings. (See below, on 2:13–15.)

[1] See Caird, p.178, and his *The Language and Imagery of the Bible* (Duckworth, 1980), pp.191 ff., and *Principalities and Powers: A Study in Pauline Theology* (OUP, 1956), pp.1–30. See also Moule, p.65, and Rowland, *The Open Heaven*, chs. 4, 5. The background belief, as expressed in the (later) work of Pseudo-Dionysius, is well discussed in C. S. Lewis, *The Discarded Image* (CUP, 1964), pp.70 ff.

[2] It is for this reason that Paul has to explain, in 1 Cor. 2:8, how the 'rulers of this age' came to crucify their Lord. They did not recognize him, he says, otherwise they would not have acted as they did.

[3] See B. J. Walsh and J. R. Middleton, *The Transforming Vision: Shaping a Christian Worldview* (IVP/USA, 1984), pp.64 f.

No power structures are, however, independent of Christ: for *all things were created by him and for him*. Again 'all things' has the article, so that we might translate it as 'the totality'. 'By him' is, this time, properly '*through* him'; 'for him' is properly '*to* him'. 'Were created' is, this time, a perfect tense ('have been created') in contrast to the aorist ('were created') at the start of the verse. The difference is that, whereas before Paul referred to the initial act of creation, he here refers to the *result* of that initial act: 'all things *have been brought into being* through him and to him'. The weight of the sentence falls, therefore, on to the final phrase 'to him'. Creation, called into existence for the sake of Christ, exists in the present in order to give him glory. Verse 16 thus moves the thought of the poem from the past (Christ as agent of creation) to the present (Christ as the one to whom the world owes allegiance) and to the future (Christ whose sovereignty will become universal). Though the powers are now in rebellion, he remains their true Lord. This is confirmed by the next stage, the first of the two short central sections of the poem.

17. Paul now sums up his statement of Christ as the intermediary of creation, before setting in parallel to this the fact of his work in the new creation. *He* (NIV omits the 'and' at the start of the line, thus losing the exact parallel with 18a) *is before all things, and in him all things hold together*. 'Before', like 'firstborn' earlier, is ambiguous, and probably refers again to primacy of both time and rank. The second clause, asserting that the world is now sustained and upheld by Christ, transfers to him one more aspect of 'wisdom' thought (see Wisdom 1:7; Ecclus. 43:26; and in the NT *cf*. Heb. 1:3). The verb, again, is in the perfect, indicating that 'everything' has held together in him and continues to do so. Through him the world is sustained, prevented from falling into chaos. No creature is autonomous. All are God's servants (Ps. 119:91) and dependents (Ps. 104).

18. It is to this Jesus Christ, none other, that the Colossians now belong in belonging to the church. This is the moment when, according to the careful structure of the poem, the thought moves from creation to new creation. Paul starts where the Colossians are, as members of the one world-wide people of

God. If God's people are the new humanity, the metaphor of a human body is utterly appropriate to express not only mutual interdependence (as in Rom. 12:5; 1 Cor. 12:12ff.) but also, as here, an organic and dependent relation to Christ himself. Hence: *And he is the head of the body, the church.* Paul, as is well known, is good at mixing his metaphors (see, *e.g.*, Eph. 4:14, with the comments of Caird[1]): he is also apparently good at adapting them to fresh uses.[2]

Paul has been exploring the different meanings of the Hebrew *rēshith* ('firstborn', 'sum-total', 'head'), and he now reaches the final stage: *he is the beginning and* (there is no word for 'and' in the Greek, and it might have been better not to add it, but to leave the next clause as an explanation of, not an addition to, 'the beginning') *the firstborn from among the dead.* This assertion dominates the remainder of the poem. The word 'beginning' is too thin to do justice to *archē*, which means 'first principle', 'source', 'creative initiative', and again indicates priority in both time and rank. (It is actually the singular noun from which is derived *archai*, rulers, as in v.16 and 2:15.) This part of the poem refers particularly to Christ's rule over the final great enemies of mankind, sin and death. With Jesus' resurrection, the new age has dawned. The new man has emerged from among the old humanity, whose life he had shared, whose pain and sin he had borne. For Paul, as throughout the Bible, sin and death were inextricably linked, so that Christ's victory over the latter signalled his defeat of the former (see Rom. 5:12–21; 1 Cor. 15:12–28). 'Firstborn' here, particularly when taken closely with *archē* in the sense of 'beginning', implies that Christ's resurrection, though presently unique, will be acted out by a great company of others. Those Jews who expected a resurrection from the dead (certainly the Pharisees, and quite possibly many others) had seen it as a large-scale, single event at the end of time. Paul, however, believed that God brought forward the inauguration of the 'age to come', the age of resurrection, into the midst of the 'present age', in order that the power of the new age might be unleashed upon the world while there was still time for the

---

[1]Caird, p.77.
[2]Many scholars suggest that 'the church' is the author's addition to the hypothetical original poem, but this is quite unwarranted: see the article referred to in n.1, p.64, above.

world to be saved.

Jesus' resurrection was thus accomplished *so that in everything he might have the supremacy.* That which he was by right he became in fact. God's plan is not merely to sum up the old creation, but to inaugurate the new creation, in and through him. The paradox of Christ's being 'before all things' (v.17) and yet *becoming* pre-eminent in his resurrection is to be explained on the basis of Philippians 2:5–11. The exaltation of Christ after his work on the cross gives him, publicly, the status which he always in fact enjoyed as of right.[1] The puzzle is caused by sin: though always Lord by right, he must become Lord in fact, by defeating sin and death. Compare Romans 1:3–4: Jesus was 'Son of God' even while being 'a descendant of David as to his human nature' (it is as Son of God that he dies on the cross, Rom. 8:3, *etc.*); in his resurrection this Sonship was powerfully, and publicly, demonstrated. The 'so that' in our present passage implies that behind Jesus' resurrection there stands the divine purpose, which is now explained as a purpose of reconciling love.

19–20. Just as verse 16 explains the appropriateness of what was said about Christ in verse 15, so verses 19–20 explain the appropriateness of verse 18b ('who is the beginning . . .'). Paul here expresses evocatively and colourfully what in 2 Corinthians 5:19 he stated bluntly ('God was reconciling the world to himself in Christ'): *For God was pleased to have all his fulness dwell in him, and through him to reconcile to himself all things, whether things on earth or things in heaven, by making peace through his blood, shed on the cross.* About this difficult little passage there are five things to be said.

i. There is no word for 'God' in the original of verse 19, but the grammatical subject ('fulness') must be a circumlocution for 'God in all his fulness' (see 2:9)'[2] It is appropriate that Christ should hold pre-eminence, because God in all his fullness was pleased to take up permanent residence (this is the best way of taking the Greek verb) in him. The full divinity of the man Jesus

[1]See my article, ' 'αρπαγμός and the meaning of Phil. 2:5–11', forthcoming in *JTS*.
[2]See Caird, pp.180 f. 'Fulness' here is certainly not (as has sometimes been suggested) a gnostic technical term for something other than God himself.

is stated without any implication that there are two Gods. It is the one God, in all his fullness, who dwells in him.

ii. The sequence 'in him . . . through him . . . to him . . .' echoes the same sequence in verse 16. This deliberate balance has created a problem of ambiguity, it being unclear whether the repeated 'him' refers to God or to Christ. The answer is probably that the final 'him' is to be taken as a contraction of 'himself' (*auton* in place of *heauton*), a verbal switch not without parallel.[1] God dwelt fully in Christ in order to reconcile all things to himself (*i.e.* to God) through him (*i.e.* Christ).

iii. In rearranging the order of phrases (see the full layout of the poem above), NIV has omitted the awkward extra phrase 'through him', which occurs in most manuscripts after the words 'his cross' and before 'whether the things on earth or the things in heaven'. But the phrase, easy to omit in copying but odd to add, should probably be retained. It re-emphasizes the fact that reconciliation was achieved through Christ alone.

iv. In what way are 'all things' reconciled to God through the cross? This question breaks down into three more: (a) how does Jesus' death effect reconciliation between God and his human creatures? (b) does 'all things' include the non-human creation? and (c) does it imply automatic salvation for all human beings?

(a) There is no problem, from the vantage-point of other Pauline statements (*e.g.* 2 Cor. 5:21), in answering this first question. On the cross, God took upon himself that which stood as a barrier between himself and his human creatures, *i.e.* sin. The worst that sin can do is to kill: dying, Jesus exhausted its power. The word 'blood' also suggests the ideas of the sacrifice which makes peace between God and man and of God's new covenant, which stands at the heart of the new creation. (See further on 1:22; 2:11–15, where this summary statement of the achievement of the cross is considerably amplified.)

(b) What, then, is the scope of this new creation? Because humanity plays the key role in the ordering of God's world, human reconciliation will lead to the restoration of creation, just as human sin led to creation's fall (compare Rom. 8:19ff.). At present, as Paul in prison knew only too well, the world as a

[1] See Moule, pp. 169 f.

whole remains unaware of the reconciliation achieved on the cross, of the fact that God will eventually remake the world and its power structures so that they reflect his glory instead of human arrogance. That is why he can speak both of the reconciliation of the 'powers' and also of God's victory in Christ over them as hostile forces (2:15). God plans for an eventual complete harmony, new heavens and new earth. All evil is to be destroyed through the cosmic outworking of the crucifixion: all creation is to be transformed in the cosmic results of the resurrection.

(c) The process of reconciliation between God and man, however, does not simply happen by some automatic process. Paul clearly believed that it was possible for human beings to reject God's offer of salvation, and that at the last judgment some, having done so, would thereby be themselves rejected (see Rom. 1:18 – 2:16; 14:10; 2 Cor. 5:10; 2 Thes. 1:5–10).[1] Since he never tells us how he would harmonize this with the reconciliation of 'all things', it is risky to guess what he might have said. But the present passage, and the parallel in 2 Corinthians 5, suggest two comments. First, he is emphasizing the universal *scope* of God's reconciling purposes; nothing less than a total new creation is envisaged. Secondly, 'reconciliation', the re-establishing of a mutual relationship, cannot occur 'automatically' in the world of human relations from which the metaphor is drawn. In theological terms, reconciliation occurs 'when someone is in Christ' (2 Cor. 5:17), which elsewhere (*e.g.* Rom. 3:21–31; 6:1–11; Gal. 3:26–29) is correlated clearly with faith and baptism. The expansion of our present passage in Colossians 2:9–12 suggests that this is the right approach. See also the commentary on 3:6, below.

v. The extraordinary events of incarnation and cross were not a *faute de mieux*, undertaken with reluctance or merely because there was no other possible course. God not only acted in this way: he 'took pleasure in' doing so. In taking human flesh in order to bring creation to its climax (1:15–17), he fulfils the eternal purpose whereby he made humanity to be master of the

---

[1]Attempts to take Rom. 5:12–21 or 11:25 ff. in a contrary sense simply fail: see my articles in *Churchman* 89, 1975, pp.197–212 and *Themelios* 4, 1979, pp. 54–58.

world. As he had been 'pleased to dwell' on Mount Zion,[1] so he is now 'pleased to dwell' among his people in human form (compare Jn. 1:14). Behind the mystery of sin, then, there stands the loving wisdom of God. In making a world which he could appropriately enter, he made man and woman in his own image. The creation of such beings entailed the possibility that they would rebel against him. Such rebellion could not baffle or perplex him, nor confound his purposes: it would evoke that quality above all others of which he had no lack, namely, the generous love expressed on the cross. He came, therefore, to defeat sin in the territory it had made its own, that of Adam, of human flesh and blood. Reconciliation, effected through the death of the Son, reveals most clearly the love of the Father (Rom. 5:6–10). It is this revelation that calls forth the praises of heaven, to which Paul now invites the Colossians to join their voices.

We are now in a position to survey the poem in its totality, and to assess the contribution it makes to the developing thought of the letter. The Colossian Christians (and their modern counterparts) are to thank God, because in Jesus Christ he has revealed himself to be the one God of all the earth, the Creator and Redeemer of all. He is not one more rival (specifically, a Jewish one) to the gods of paganism. He reigns supreme over all. He has given himself to his world in loving self-sacrifice, to create out of sinful humanity a people for his own possession, with the intention of eventually bringing the entire universe into a new order and harmony. All this he has done in and through Jesus, his Son, his own perfect human self-expression.

Out of the many points here which could be developed further, Paul highlights two.

First (2:6–23), Jesus has taken the role assigned by Judaism to 'Wisdom' and the law. No Christian should think to consolidate his or her freedom from the spiritual tyrannies of the world by taking on the 'extra' protection of the Jewish law. Monotheism, election, Torah, the three pillars of Judaism, have all been redefined in and through Jesus Christ. Possessing him –

---

[1]See Ps. 67:17, LXX (EVV 68:16); cf. further Lohse, p.58.

better, being possessed by him – the Christian is already 'complete' (2:10, AV). Second (3:5 – 4:6), the new life in Christ is nothing less than the beginning of the new creation. And, if new creation, new humanity. Christians already share in the new age which began on Easter Day. This is worked out in terms of practical holiness, which does not thwart or cramp full humanity, but facilitates and enhances it.

If we wished to apply what Paul has here given us to further questions relating to the last quarter of the twentieth century, we might do so in a variety of ways, recognizing that such matters are not questions simply of exegesis, but of possible applications of exegesis. Thus, for instance, monotheism, often taken for granted, is once again a live issue. To assert today that the one Creator God has revealed himself fully and finally in Jesus Christ is to risk criticism on the grounds of arrogance or intolerance. The mission of the church, however, does not commit Christians to the proposition that there is no truth to be found in other religions. Colossians 1:16 implies that all philosophies or religions which have some 'fit' with the created world will thereby reflect in some ways the truth of God. It does not, however, imply that they are therefore, as they stand, doorways into the *new* creation. That place, according to 1:18, is Christ's alone.

A further application concerns the church's task in the world. There is no sphere of existence over which Jesus is not sovereign, in virtue of his role both in creation (1:16–17) and in reconciliation (1:18–20). There can be no dualistic division between some areas which he rules and others which he does not. 'There is no neutral ground in the universe: every square inch, every split second, is claimed by God and counterclaimed by Satan.'[1] The task of evangelism is therefore best understood as the proclamation that Jesus is already Lord, that in him God's new creation has broken into history, and that all people are therefore summoned to submit to him in love, worship and obedience. The logic of this message requires that those who announce it should be seeking to bring Christ's Lordship to bear

[1]See C. S. Lewis, 'Christianity and Culture' in *Christian Reflections*, ed. W. Hooper (Bles, 1967), p.33 (2nd edn, Fount Paperbacks, 1981, p.52).

on every area of human and worldly existence. Christians must work to help create conditions in which human beings, and the whole created world, can live as God always intended. There is a whole range of ethical norms which God built into his world: respect for persons and property, maintenance of family life and of the ecological order of creation, justice between individuals and groups. Christians must be in the forefront of those working to promote such causes. Many opportunities to speak about Jesus will occur in the undertaking of such work, as it becomes clear that the gospel provides a coherent and satisfying underpinning for those standards which uphold and enhance a truly human life.

The basic target of Paul's polemic, the main thing that the gospel was bound to attack, was idolatry. Anything put in the place of the one God of all the earth becomes an idol, be it never so useful, beautiful or sacred. Even the God-given Torah could become an idol: how much more the man-made political and economic systems of Paul's world or ours. To apply the gospel to the idolatry of our modern world will take more prayer, discernment, humility and wisdom than it is usually given. Not to apply it in this way is implicitly to deny it.

Colossians 1:15–20 gives the church not merely an exalted view of Jesus, and hence of humanity, but of God and his world. God, man and the world are each now to be understood in relation to Jesus Christ. He makes the invisible God visible; he fulfils the Father's reconciling purpose on the cross; he is the Father's agent in creation and redemption. He is the truly human being,[1] the true Image of God. He is Lord of old and new creation, being in himself the beginning of the latter, the first created being to attain the state of perfection which will one day be shared by 'all things in heaven and on earth'. It is this Lord that the Colossians have come to worship, his 'image' that they will one day fully share (3:10). This is the fact to which Paul now turns, applying the poem to the young church he is addressing.

c. New creation in Colosse (1:21–23). The reconciliation just

---

[1]See the masterly explanation of this subject, in relation to modern human problems, in S. C. Neill, *A Genuinely Human Existence* (Doubleday, 1959).

mentioned is not a strange new truth to the Colossians. They have already experienced it. Paul here outlines their former plight, the means of their rescue, and their consequent present hope. This statement ties verses 13–23 with the thanksgiving of verses 3–8, points forward to the appeal of chapter 2, and enables Paul to work round to the detailed introduction of himself which follows immediately in 1:24 – 2:5.

21. The Colossians, then, *were once alienated from God.* NIV, by adding 'from God', brings out the sense, which is not that of Ephesians 2:12 (where the estrangement is between Gentiles and the Old Covenant people of God), but is nearer to Ephesians 4:18. Made for obedient fellowship with God, humanity since the fall is somehow out of order, God's design having been spoilt by sin. The result is that *(you) were enemies in your minds because of your evil behaviour.* The Greek is not quite so clear as appears from NIV's 'because'. It is not simply that habitual wrongdoing has turned the mind away from God. Nor is the word translated 'mind' (*dianoia*) strictly the mind itself, but the way it works, the processes of understanding and intellect. Thought and act are both tainted, each pushing the other into further corruption, in a mirror image of 1:9–10 (see above). The best comment on 1:21 is perhaps the sequence of thought in Romans 1:21–32. Wrong thinking leads to vice, vice to further mental corruption, so that the mind, still not totally ignorant of God's standards, finds itself applauding evil.

22. Paul now applies verse 20 to the problem of verse 21, and concludes that God *has now reconciled you by Christ's physical body through death to present you holy in his sight.* He does not say that God's action in Christ, and the Colossian's acceptance of the gospel, have automatically and instantly made them perfect. Having been given a new life, they must behave in accordance with it. This they can do only because of the reconciliation (between themselves, as pagan sinners, and the Creator God, the God of Israel) which was achieved on the cross.

But how? NIV, by simplifying 'the body of his flesh' into 'Christ's physical body', has somewhat obscured a collocation of tricky technical terms. For Paul, the word 'flesh' (*sarx*) frequently describes not merely the physical aspect of human nature, but humanity as it opposes God. 'Body', on the other hand, which also describes man as a totality, not merely as a physical entity, is morally neutral. What, then, does 'the body of his flesh' mean, and how is it the means of reconciliation?

Two parallel passages, both in Romans, will help us here. In 7:4 Paul writes 'you died to the law through the body of Christ', and in 8:3 he says that God, 'sending his own Son in the likeness of sinful flesh and as a sin-offering,[1] condemned sin in the flesh' (RSV). The context of both passages within Romans 5 – 8 as a whole, coupled with the reference in Colossians 1:18 to Christ as 'the head of the body', suggests the following train of thought:

(a) Jesus, as Messiah, represents, and is fully identified with, his people. He shares their 'fleshly' existence, so that, though himself without sin, he takes sin's consequences on himself, becoming subject to death.

(b) Jesus is also fully identified with God (1:19; this identification is further described in 2:9 as *sōmatikōs*, bodily).

(c) In Jesus, therefore, God identified himself with the sins of humanity. The cross is simply the outworking of this explosive meeting between the holy God and human sin.

(d) Those who are members of Jesus' 'body' thus find their sin already condemned in him, and themselves reconciled to God. Jesus has risen from the dead, as the first of a large family whose sins, having done their worst in producing his death, are left behind in his life beyond death (1:18; see Rom. 6:7–11; 8:29). It is this line of thought, I suggest, that Paul has expressed compactly in the first half of verse 22.

The reconciliation thus effected has a definite and attractive aim in view. God's purpose is *to present you holy in his sight, without blemish*. The words translated 'present', 'in his sight' and 'without blemish' all evoke the language of Jewish sacrificial ritual. (Sacrifice had to be 'without blemish': so, physically speaking, did the priest who offered it.) Paul may therefore be hinting at a sacrificial metaphor, though it could hardly be fully stated, since it would imply that God was offering a sacrifice to

[1]See my article 'The Meaning of *peri hamartias* in Rom. 8.3' in *Studia Biblica 1978* vol. 3, ed. E. A. Livingstone (JSOT Press, 1980), pp.453–459.

himself. Better, therefore, to leave it as a hint.

As often, Paul here mixes his metaphors, adding *and free from accusation*. This indicates not merely a legal setting, where a defendant might, like the woman in John 8:10–11, find himself without accuser. The other New Testament uses of the word[1] suggest the context of community life in general, where not even casual gossip will be able to find a word to say against the person in question. NIV takes 'without blemish' and 'free from accusation' as explaining the meaning of 'holy'. RSV, which sets all three terms in parallel, is to be preferred, (a) because holiness is more than the sum of these two negatives and (b) because there is an 'and' preceding 'without blemish'. When God looks at Christians (Paul is saying), he desires that they should be holy *and* without blemish *and* without reproach.

God's purpose, then, is to create a holy people in Christ. This he *has* done in principle, by dealing with sin on the cross and thus already achieving reconciliation. This he *is* doing in practice, by refashioning their lives according to the pattern of the perfect life, that of Christ (see 3:10). This he *will* do in the future, when that work is complete and the church enjoys fully that which at present it awaits in hope. The present process, which begins with patient Christian living and ends with the resurrection itself, will result in Christians being presented without shame or fear before God, as glad subjects before their king.

23. This promise, like most, has a condition. The hope holds good, if Christians hold on to it: *if you continue in your faith, established and firm, not moved from the hope held out in the gospel.* Paul knows that true Christian faith is the beginning of a life which, given by God, will be brought to completion by him (Phil. 1:6). He also knows that genuine faith is seen in patient and steadfast day-to-day Christian living, while counterfeit faith, so hard in its early stages to distinguish from the real thing, withers and dies. From God's point of view, genuine faith is assured of continuing to the end. From the human point of view, Christians discover whether their faith is of the genuine sort only by patient perseverance, encouraged (*cf.* Rom. 5:1–5)

---

[1] 1 Tim. 3:10; Tit. 1:6–7; see also, in a similar context to our present one, 1 Cor. 1:8.

by the Christian hope. There is here almost certainly a deliberate echo of 1:4–5.

The verb 'continue' (*epimenein*) often has the sense, in constructions like this, of remaining in a place or locality. It makes good sense here to take it in this way, and to see 'the faith' as a 'place' (perhaps, as we say, 'the Christian faith') where Christians must 'remain' rather than just the activity of believing. 'The faith' includes that activity, but goes beyond it to indicate the content of what is believed, and perhaps also the whole Christian way of life.

The words 'established' and 'firm' refer to the security, respectively, of foundations and superstructure. Painstaking work at every stage of building results in an unmovable structure. This metaphor evokes not merely the secular building trade but the founding of the people of God.[1] And the 'place' where this structure is located is the gospel itself, the proclamation of Jesus Christ as Lord (see above, on 1:3ff.).

Having narrowed his horizons from the world as a whole to the church in Colosse, Paul broadens them again, to show the young church once more where it fits into the divine plan. *This is the gospel that you heard,* he writes, *and that has been proclaimed to every creature under heaven.* Referring again to 1:3–8, he claims that the Colossian church, in hearing the gospel, has joined an audience that includes every creature on the earth (echoing 1:6 and 1:16). This is an extraordinary statement. Whenever we date this letter, Paul knew perfectly well when writing it that the vast majority of people in the known world of his day had not even heard the name of Jesus. What, then, did he mean?

We appear to be faced with three possible answers. (a) Either Paul is referring to a proclamation of the gospel which takes place in and through a revelation in the world of created 'nature' itself: or (b) he could be thinking of a single proclamation of the gospel (in the sense of an announcement of Christ's Lordship) which, made in advance of its verbal declaration to human beings, was somehow made known to the other orders of creation: or (c) he intended this claim to be taken in an anticipatory sense; that, in Christ himself and in the fact of the Gentile

[1] Ps. 48:8; Is. 14:32; 44:28; Hg. 2:18; Zc. 4:9; 8:9.

84

mission, the gospel had *in principle* already been preached world-wide.

The first two interpretations seem unlikely. Even if Paul did believe in a revelation of God the Father in the world of nature (some have denied this, but it seems clear enough in Rom. 1:19ff., not to mention Acts 14:17; 17:24ff.), he never suggests that the gospel itself, the good news about Jesus Christ, has been made known in this way. Nor does the idea of an independent proclamation to the non-human creation find any echoes elsewhere in his writings. Nor would it be clear how he, Paul, could become a minister of such a proclamation, as he says in the next phrase. Romans 10:18, though sometimes read in this way, refers in context to Paul's own Gentile mission, seen from God's point of view as a single world-wide proclamation.

All of this strengthens the view that the third answer is correct. The aorist tense should strictly speaking be translated not 'that has been preached' but 'that was preached'. The verb *kēryssein*, one of Paul's regular words for his own activity (as in the next clause), supports the idea of a proclamation made to human beings rather than the notion of an instantaneous announcement made directly to the non-human orders of creation. God has, in principle, announced the gospel to every creature under heaven. Although, however, the proclamation is made to human beings, we would be quite wrong, in view of 1:16, 18 and 20, and the emphatic reiteration of 'everything' there and elsewhere in Colossians, to limit its *effects* to them.[1] From whales to waterfalls, the whole created order has in principle been reconciled to God. Like a sovereign making a proclamation and sending off his heralds to bear it to the distant corners of his empire, God has in Jesus Christ proclaimed once and for all that the world which he made has been reconciled to him. His heralds, scurrying off to the ends of the earth with the news, are simply agents, messengers, of this one antecedent authoritative proclamation.

And *Paul* is among them. He has *become a servant of* this gospel, this message. He uses the same word, *diakonos*, of him-

---

[1]See M. Barth 'Christ and All Things', in *Paul and Paulinism: Essays in Honour of C. K. Barrett*, ed. M. D. Hooker and S. G. Wilson (SPCK, 1982), pp.160–172, against *e.g.* Lohse, pp.66 f.

self that he had used of Epaphras in 1:7. It does not carry a technical sense of particular church office. It merely describes Paul, and Epaphras, as 'stewards' or 'administrators', set apart to 'distribute' the gospel much as the seven 'deacons' in Acts 6 were set apart to distribute food.

With this, Paul concludes his long description of his thanksgiving and prayer. He has managed to include all the main themes he wishes to develop, and to set them in a context which shows that they are not mere abstract ideas or theories, but part of the living faith which he and the Colossians now share.

C. PAUL'S MINISTRY AND HIS REASONS FOR WRITING (1:24 – 2:5)

Paul now completes his introduction of himself, before launching into the reasoned appeal of 2:6 – 4:6. He does so with a remarkably full description of his ministry, in order apparently to ensure that the Colossians, who had until now only heard of him second-hand, would understand his reasons for writing. Having put them on the map of the divine purposes in Christ (1:21–23), Paul now places himself on that same map. His writing at the present time is not an odd or arrogant venture. His whole ministry – his suffering, preaching, teaching, hard work and prayer – has had them in view for some time, and this letter is simply one more facet of his total God-given work, which includes responsibility for them.

Any suggestion that his writing might be an act of presumption (attempting to intrude where another had first claim) is forestalled by the centrality of Christ in this passage, which is thereby linked directly to the great theme that has occupied chapter 1 up to this point. Paul's sufferings are to be understood, in some strange sense, as not his own, but Christ's. His preaching and teaching are God's means of accomplishing that which he is doing in Christ. His (Paul's) hard work is accomplished only because Christ is at work in him. And, if Christ is his motivating and energizing power, Christ is also his goal. Christ's body is the beneficiary of his sufferings (1:24). Christ's indwelling in his people is their hope of glory (1:27). Maturity in Christ is Paul's ambition for every Christian (1:28). Good order in Christ is what he is glad to see in the young church (2:5). Christ himself *is* God's secret plan (1:27; 2:2), revealed in every aspect of Paul's work.

By introducing himself in this way Paul shows where his true credentials lie. He explains in the first paragraph (1:24–29) the nature of his own ministry in Christ; in the second (2:1–5), how this ministry relates to the church in Colosse. He thus follows the pattern he has already used in 1:15–20, 21–23: new creation in Christ, new creation in Colosse.

i. Paul's ministry in Christ (1:24–29)

24. Elsewhere, too, Paul declares that he rejoices in his sufferings (*e.g.* Rom. 5:3). The idea that this suffering is somehow endured on behalf of the people to whom he writes is not unknown (2 Cor. 1:6; Eph. 3:13; *cf.* 2 Tim. 2:10). But this verse goes further. It seems to tie Paul's sufferings to the sufferings of Christ himself, and in so doing raises a number of problems. How can Paul claim what surely belongs to Christ alone, namely, the vocation to suffer on behalf of others? NIV has softened this emphasis by its rendering, *Now I rejoice in what was suffered for you*. It is true that the word *mou* ('my'), qualifying 'sufferings' in the original, is lacking from most manuscripts, but RSV in supplying it ('Now I rejoice in my sufferings for your sake') has only brought out the force of the definite article before 'sufferings', taken in the light of the whole verse and of Ephesians 3:13. How, particularly, can Paul claim that in his sufferings he is able to *fill up in my flesh what is still lacking in regard to Christ's afflictions, for the sake of his body, which is the church*? How can there be anything lacking in the sufferings of Christ? Supporters of rival theories of the atonement have always regarded this verse, or at least their opponents' handling of it, with deep suspicion. But such fears are unnecessary if we understand Paul's world of thought.

Two ideas from Paul's Jewish understanding of God's purposes help us to see what he means. First, there is *corporate Christology*, expressed in the second half of the verse by the concept of the church as Christ's body. That which is true of Christ is true also of his people. Second, there is the concept of the *Messianic woes*, which Paul alludes to also in Romans 8:18–25.[1] This latter idea, developed out of Old Testament hints by some intertestamental and Rabbinic writers, is part of the view (shared by Jesus and Paul) that world history is to be divided into two ages – the present (evil) age (*cf.* Gal. 1:4) and the age to come. When the great moment arrives for history to move from one age to the next, God's people will suffer (so it was believed) extraordinary tribulations, which were to be understood as the birthpangs of the new age (Rom. 8:22). They are to be the accompaniment, or perhaps the foreshadowing, of the appearance of the Messiah.

Paul's appropriation of this idea is, like all his reusing of Jewish material, reshaped by the facts of Jesus' death and resurrection. Instead of the old and the new ages standing as it were back to back, he understood them as overlapping. Jesus' resurrection had inaugurated the new age, but the old would continue alongside it until Jesus' second coming. The whole of the time-span between the Lord's resurrection and his return was, then, the period of the turn-around of the eras: and therefore the whole period would be characterized by 'the Messianic woes'. Such suffering, indeed, is actually regarded as evidence that the sufferers really are God's new people. That is why Paul can talk of rejoicing *in* his sufferings, as opposed to merely rejoicing in the midst of, or despite, them. Just as the Messiah was to be known by the path of suffering he freely chose – and is recognized in his risen body by the mark of the nails (Lk. 24:39; Jn. 20:20, 25, 27) – so his people are to be recognized by the sufferings they endure:

> And in the garden secretly,
> And on the cross on high,
> Should teach His brethren, and inspire
> To suffer and to die.

They are not merely imitating him. They are incorporated into his life, his paradoxical new way of life.

It is in this sense that Paul can speak of filling up the afflictions of the Messiah. He is not adding to the achievement of

---

[1] See Rowland, *The Open Heaven*, pp.156–160.

Calvary. The word 'afflictions' (*thlipsis* in the Greek) is never, in fact, used of the cross. He is merely putting into practice the principle of which Calvary was, in one sense, the supreme outworking. He understands the vocation of the church as being to suffer; he does not arrogate this privilege to himself, as though he were independent of Christ, but rightly sees that it is his precisely because it is Christ's, and so is he. This is what he means when he writes of suffering 'with Christ' (Rom. 8:17) or of sharing the fellowship of Christ's sufferings (Phil. 3:10).

That this is the correct approach to the verse is confirmed by two other considerations. First, the interchange between Christ and Paul permeates the whole paragraph, not merely this verse; see especially 1:29. Second, the parallel passages in 2 Corinthians 1:3–7 and 4:7–12 possess, in more full and hence less cryptic expression, the same combination of elements.

Paul therefore applies to himself the same pattern, of suffering on behalf of others, that was worked out on the cross. He does not think thereby to save the Colossians from their sin and its consequences. That work is already done. But he may perhaps save them some present suffering. By drawing the enemy's fire on to himself, he may allow the young church something of a respite from the fierce attacks they might otherwise be facing. There may also be here (though this is not provable) the idea of a fixed amount of suffering to be undergone in the dawning of the Messianic age. Paul delights to take as much of it as he can, in order to spare others. It is less probable, though some have suggested it, that in so doing he is hoping to hasten the Lord's return. If all these ideas sound strange to modern ears, this may be not so much due to the distance between Paul and ourselves in time and culture as because the church has forgotten how to apply to itself the fact that it is the body of the crucified Messiah.

Three details – two of exegesis, one of application – remain.

The word 'now' at the start of the verse is not, as in English, a mere transition word (roughly equivalent to 'well, then . . .'). But it is not clear whether it is (a) temporal, referring to a rejoicing which Paul has 'now', while in prison, as opposed to that which he had before, or (b) logical, referring to the fact that he can rejoice thus 'now' because of the truths he has just been

rehearsing in 1:15–20. The latter seems more probable. Paul's
reasons for rejoicing will not be removed when he is released
from prison.

Second, the word rendered 'fill up' has another preposition
attached to it (*i.e.* the first three letters of the word *antanaplēro*),
which is very difficult to bring out in translation. If my interpretation of the verse is correct, the preposition *ant(i)* will have
the effect of emphasizing that what Paul is suffering he is suffering in some way not merely on behalf of the young church
but actually instead of it.

Finally, we would be wrong to think of suffering only in terms
of the direct outward persecution that professing Christians
sometimes undergo because of their faith. The church must, it is
true, always be ready for such persecution, and must support,
in prayer and practical help, those who face it. But all Christians
will suffer for their faith in one way or another: if not outwardly,
then inwardly, through the long, slow battle with temptation or
sickness, the agonizing anxieties of Christian responsibilities for
a family or a church (Paul knew these too: see 2 Cor. 1 and 2;
1 Thes. 2:17 – 3:1), the constant doubts and uncertainties which
accompany the obedience of faith, and 'the thousand natural
shocks that flesh is heir to', taken up as they are within the call
to follow Christ. All of these, properly understood, are things to
rejoice in – not casually, flippantly or superficially, but because
they are signs that the present age is passing away, that the
people of Jesus, the Messiah, are the children of the new age,
and that the birthpangs of this new age are being worked out in
them. This knowledge about the two ages, as we shall see,
forms the basis of Paul's later appeal in 2:20 – 3:4.

25. In verse 23 Paul described himself as the servant of the
gospel. Here, with an enviable balance, he sees himself as the
servant of the church. He has a special responsibility towards
the Colossians, just as the steward of a great house might be
entrusted by his master with responsibility of attending to the
needs of his guests: *I have become its* (*i.e.* the church's) *servant by
the commission God gave me.* His task is simply stated: *to present to
you the word of God in its fullness,* or, more literally, 'to fulfil the
word of God'. We should not restrict this phrase, as NIV seems

to do, to the preaching of the 'whole counsel of God' (Acts 20:27, RSV). Nor is it a matter simply of 'making the word of God fully known', as RSV translates. 'The word of God' is, for Paul, a power let loose in the world, embodied in the true gospel message (see 1:6). It must be allowed to have its full effect, to be 'fulfilled' in that sense.

26–27. This is confirmed by Paul's further definition of 'the word of God' as *the mystery that has been kept hidden for ages and generations but is now disclosed to the saints . . .* (namely) *Christ in you, the hope of glory.* Here again we have Jewish ideas rethought in the light of the gospel. In their looking forward to the day when God would act in history to restore the fortunes of his people, some Jewish seers expressed their hopes in terms of the 'secret plans' that God was reserving for the last great day.[1] The word 'mystery' is properly to be understood against this background. It is unlikely that the word contains a veiled allusion, or an implicit challenge, to pagan mystery-cults,[2] and quite certain that it does not mean (as the English word 'mystery' often does) something merely puzzling or paradoxical. It is God's secret plan, anticipated in visions and symbols by holy men of old, and now at last unveiled before all his people ('the saints' here is not a restricted group within the church, but, as regularly, the whole people of God). We may compare 1 Corinthians 2:7: 'we speak of God's secret wisdom, a wisdom that has been hidden and that God destined for our glory before time began'.

God's secret plan is not, for Paul, a timetable of events, but a person. We see here the outworking of the Christology of 1:15–20. All that God has from the beginning planned to do he has done, and is doing, in Christ, for the sake of his people: *to them God has chosen to make known among the Gentiles the glorious riches of this mystery.* These phrases should perhaps be turned around to bring out the emphasis of the Greek: a literal translation might be 'to them God wished to make known what is the richness of the glory of this mystery among the Gentiles' (NIV seems to make 'to them' redundant by appearing to let 'among

---

[1] See Rowland, *ibid.*, pp.160–176, *etc.*

[2] Still less likely that instead of 'for ages and generations' we should translate, with RSV margin, 'from angels and men'.

the Gentiles' qualify 'make known' instead of 'this mystery'). At the centre of the mystery stands the revelation, in Christ, that God's purposes were not to be restricted to the Jews, but were to embrace the entire world. It is this fact, for Paul, that reveals the 'riches of the glory' of God's plan. God is revealed in Jesus Christ as the Lord of the *whole* world, its sovereign and loving Creator and Redeemer. Looking into his astonishing plans is – according to the metaphor Paul has used – like exploring a palace richly stocked with treasures, each one revealing more fully than the last the majesty of the owner.

Among these treasures is the fact that God's glory is to be *shared* with his people (*cf.* Rom. 5:2).[1] This *hope of glory* is a certainty because of the mystery itself, which is *Christ in you*. This could be taken as 'Christ *among* you' (the 'you' is plural), its emphasis being that of the immediately preceding phrase, 'among the Gentiles'. The fact that the Jewish Messiah has made his abode among the nations of the world shows that God intends their ultimate glorification. But, though this sense is thoroughly Pauline, it is probably better to take the phrase in the sense of Romans 8:10, where the indwelling of Christ in believers is their guarantee of resurrection. It should be noted that, although 'Christ in you' can be truly predicated of all who are 'in Christ', and vice versa, these two ideas are not the same. Christ indwells, by his Spirit, all those who, in belonging to his family, are said to be 'in him'. Romans 8:1–11 provides good examples of both ideas: so do verses 27–28 of our present passage.

28–29. Christ's design (v.22) is to 'present' his people to God, holy and without reproach. Paul's aim, derived from this, is that he may present everyone perfect in Christ. The parallel reveals again how closely Paul related God's purpose and his own vocation. It is *because* God is at work that Paul is at work. The paradox, capturing so neatly the correct balance between divine sovereignty and human responsibility in the work of Christian ministry, comes to a head in verse 29. *To this end I labour*; but, whereas human logic would see this as a statement of mere

---

[1] See the useful note on 'glory' in Caird, p.186.

human effort (and effort it is: the word used refers to uncom-
promising hard work), the higher logic of God's work in human
beings recognizes a deeper truth; *struggling with all his energy,
which so powerfully works in me, i.e.* the energy of God's Spirit at
work in Paul (the whole thought is very close to that of 1 Cor.
15:10). The word 'struggling', whose root can mean 'to compete
in the games', carries, as often in Paul, the idea of athletic
contest: Paul does not go about his work half-heartedly, hoping
vaguely that grace will fill in the gaps which he is too lazy to
work at himself. Nor, however, does he imagine that it is 'all up
to him', so that unless he burns himself out with restless,
anxious toil nothing will be achieved. He knows that God's
desire is to bring Christians to maturity, *and* that God has called
him to have a share in that work. He can therefore work hard
without the stressful motivation of either pride or fear. He thus
becomes an example of that maturity, both human and Christian, that he seeks under God to produce in others.

The work consists in *proclaiming him, i.e.* Christ. This proclamation has a twofold aspect, *admonishing and teaching everyone
with all wisdom,* and a definite goal, *so that we may present everyone
perfect in Christ.* Actually 'everyone' is repeated three times,
occurring after 'admonishing' as well. This emphasizes that
every single Christian is capable of the maturity of which Paul
speaks, since, though it involves 'knowledge' and 'wisdom',
these are not to be weighed in the scale of ordinary human
intellectual ability, but are of an altogether different order (*cf.*
1 Cor. 2:6–16). (This is not to say that this knowledge and wisdom
will not stretch the finest intellects to the very limits of their
capacities.) 'Him we proclaim': these words serve, for Christian
preachers and teachers, as a constant reminder of their central
calling, not (first and foremost) to comment on current affairs or
to alleviate human problems, good and necessary as those activities may be, but to announce that Jesus is Lord.

This announcement will, in its detailed application, include
'admonishing' as well as positive 'teaching'. The first word
(*nouthetountes*), though sometimes understood as meaning
simply 'putting into the mind', most likely includes the idea of
the setting of someone's mind into proper order, with the
implication that it has been in some way out of joint. Positive

93

teaching may not be enough: there is no telling what muddles Christian minds will get into from time to time, and part of the task of one who proclaims Christ is to straighten out confusions, to search for and tie together correctly the loose ends of half-grasped ideas, so that the positive teaching may not be instantly distorted upon reception, but may be properly understood, appreciated and lived out. Then it is that the goal of maturity (not 'perfection' in the sense of sinlessness, as Phil. 3:13-14 makes clear) may be in sight. This goal is possible 'in Christ': the Image of God himself now lives in his people by his Spirit (1:8), working secretly until their life and his are indistinguishable in their basic character, in true humanity (1:27; 3:10).

ii. Paul's ministry to the Colossians (2:1-5)

2:1-2a. The reason Paul has told them all this (2:1 should, despite NIV's omission, begin with the word 'for', as in RSV) is that *I want you to know how much I am struggling for you and for those at Laodicea,*[1] *and for all who have not met me personally.* It is important that the new Christians in Colosse, and for that matter at nearby Laodicea (who had had their own letter: see the commentary on 4:16) should realize that, though they have never met Paul, he has long been working on their behalf. The word 'struggling', continuing the athletic metaphor of 1:29, re-emphasizes that this has been no light task.

Paul then elaborates further the meaning of maturity. *My purpose is that they may be encouraged in heart and united in love, so that they may have the full riches of complete understanding.* NIV has here slightly obscured the relation of the clauses: 'united' properly governs not only 'in love' but also the next phrase, which literally means 'and unto all the wealth of conviction of understanding'. In other words, while the process of knitting together the church into a united body clearly includes the growth of love, it also includes the growth, on the part of the whole community, of that proper understanding of the gospel which leads to the rich blessings of a settled conviction and assurance. Living in a loving and forgiving community will

[1]Some MSS add 'and Hierapolis'.

assist growth in understanding, and vice versa, as truth is confirmed in practice and practice enables truth to be seen in action and so to be fully grasped (*cf.* 1:9–11). All of this promotes the encouragement, comfort and strengthening of the heart, regarded metaphorically then as now as the seat of affections and the mainspring of actions.

2b–3. But what does 'complete understanding' mean? Paul explains: he is working *in order that they may know the mystery of God, namely, Christ,*[1] *in whom are hidden all the treasures of wisdom and knowledge.* This is both a comfort and a challenge to Christians. They do not need to look for wisdom or knowledge elsewhere than to the one they already possess, but at the same time they have a long way to go if they are to explore and make their own the rich inheritance they have entered into. For God's 'mystery' see above, on 1:26. Here the idea is spelt out in terms of the Christology of 1:15–20. Christ sums up in himself all that the Jews predicated of 'Wisdom' (*cf.* Pr. 2:1–8, whose LXX translation is echoed several times in our present passage). Christ himself *is* 'the mystery of God': not just a clue or a key to it, as though it were something other than himself, a proposition which, however true, remained abstract. Everything we might want to ask about God and his purposes can and must now be answered – this is the force of the verse – with reference to the crucified and risen Jesus, the Messiah. Paul's repeated descriptions of such understanding as 'riches' or 'treasure' invite his readers to explore it with eagerness.

4–5. *I tell you this* – that is, I make these central and all-embracing claims – *so that no-one may deceive you by fine-sounding arguments.* Paul does not say that the Colossians have already been deceived, but from long experience he knows that a work of grace is followed by an attack from the enemy, and that one regular form this attack may take is the clever plausibility of teaching near enough to the truth to be apparently respectable and far enough away from it to be devastating in its effect on

---

[1]There is, not surprisingly, considerable MS variation at this point. NIV has rightly adopted the reading which, by its startling brevity and high Christology, more easily explains the others (see Metzger, p.622).

individuals and congregations. This is the first definite indication Paul gives that his letter is going to contain negative as well as positive teaching. Again the note struck – as frequently in Colossians – is the importance of clear and straight *thinking*. It is by spurious *arguments* that such teachers win the day, and valid arguments, based on the centrality of Jesus Christ, are the proper weapons with which to meet them.

Paul, himself a master theologian, assures the Colossians that he is undertaking this task on their behalf in writing this letter: *for though I am absent from you in body, I am present with you in spirit (cf.* 1 Cor. 5:3; 1 Thes. 2:17). At the moment he is happy with what he sees: *and delight to see how orderly you are and how firm your faith in Christ is.* 'Orderly' and 'firm' are most probably military metaphors: the church is drawn up in proper battle array with a solid wall of defence, namely, its faith in Christ. Paul is there in spirit, like a general inspecting the troops before a battle. It is possible that the two words joined together in NIV's 'delighting to see' should in fact be kept separate:[1] Paul is rejoicing not merely because of the church's proper battle preparations but, as in 1:3ff., because of the many things that God has accomplished among them. He is glad in the Lord to be with them, and is keeping careful watch on their readiness for the spiritual, and consequently intellectual, warfare into which they may shortly be plunged.

III. THE APPEAL FOR CHRISTIAN MATURITY (2:6 – 4:6)

We come now to the central section of the epistle. It has certain clear paragraph divisions, but one should not think that each paragraph deals with a separate watertight topic. The whole section is bound together by various important themes – most noticeably, of course, the centrality of Christ – and is thereby integrated also with the long introduction we have just studied.

The line of thought moves by a process of growth and development. The opening statement (2:6–7) serves as a sum-

---

[1]See, *e.g.*, Williams, p.80: against, *e.g.*, O'Brien, pp.98 f.

mary of all that is to come.[1] (The main subdivision falls at the start of ch. 3: it would be too simple to see 2:8–23 as negative teaching and 3:1 – 4:6 as positive, though there would be some truth in that.) 2:8–12 provides the initial warning against false teaching and the basic reason for opposing it: having been baptized into Christ, Christians are already complete in him. 2:13–15 applies this to the Colossians' situation, as Gentile Christians for whom Christ's victory on the cross means freedom from the tyranny of alien forces. 2:16–19, in turn, applies this latter point: no-one can deny the Colossians their status within the Body of Christ. 2:20–23 then warns against the false means of attaining holiness that such a rival scheme might promote, and 3:1–4, balancing this, sets out the true alternative. Having died with Christ and been raised with him (2:20 – 3:4 thus draws out the implications of 2:12), Christians are not to be governed by the kind of rules that properly belong in the old age. Instead, they are to live the life appropriate to the new age. This will mean (3:5–11) putting to death the behaviour which belongs to their former life, and (3:12–17) replacing it with that which characterizes the true humanity given in Christ. This truly human behaviour is to characterize both home life and Christian witness before the world (3:18 – 4:6).

This general summary holds true, I believe, whatever view is taken of the particular teaching Paul is opposing. Of that much-debated question I have given an account in the Introduction (see above, pp. 23–30). I there suggested that the teaching in question is not (as often supposed) a strange amalgam of Judaism and paganism. It is in fact Judaism itself, portrayed (as we saw that it sometimes portrayed itself) in the guise of 'just another religion', which might appear attractive to those who, having left paganism behind to join the church, might be tempted to see Judaism as the fulfilment of Christianity instead of vice versa.[2] I believe that the detailed exegesis of the present passage will provide strong support for this view. At the same time I trust that if any remain unpersuaded by my arguments, and prefer to adopt one or other of the alternative analyses

[1]Compare, *e.g.*, Rom. 7:5–6 in relation to 7:7 – 8:11.
[2]See Houlden, pp.189, 193, 195 f.

(there is at present no scholarly consensus whatever on the matter), they will still find this section of the commentary helpful.

A. INTRODUCTION: CONTINUE IN CHRIST (2:6-7)

6-7. These two verses sum up neatly the message of the entire letter. In them Paul draws together the awesome Christology of the introduction and the practical teaching that is to be based on it: *So then, just as you received Christ Jesus as Lord, continue to live in him.* The emphasis, in the light of the letter's long introduction, must be: it is *this* Christ (God's Image, God's Wisdom, God's Mystery) that you have 'received' in becoming Christians. Moreover, this Christ is none other than the crucified and risen Jesus, now exalted as Lord. Each of the three parts of the phrase 'Christ Jesus . . . Lord' is thus to be given its proper weight.

But what does Paul mean by 'receiving' Christ? Here we must guard against anachronism. In popular language today the phrase 'to receive Christ' often expresses that conception of becoming a Christian which focuses on the new believer's invitation to Jesus Christ to enter into his or her heart and life. Such an idea is powerful and evocative, and relates closely to the Pauline doctrine of Christ dwelling in the hearts of his people (Rom. 8:9-10; Eph. 3:17). The difficulty here is that Paul's phrase 'to receive Christ' almost certainly carries quite different overtones. The verb 'receive' (*paralambanō*) is sometimes used in a technical sense, taken over from Judaism, referring to the transmission of teaching from one person or generation to another: compare 'just as you were taught' in the next verse.[1] There are, in addition, several hints in the passage to suggest that he has the moment, and significance, of baptism in mind. The phrase 'Christ Jesus the Lord' corresponds closely to the early confessional formula 'Jesus Christ is Lord' (Phil. 2:11; *cf.* Rom. 10:9; 1 Cor. 12:3), which converts would profess at their baptism. Paul mentions baptism explicitly in verse 12, and various

[1] See Bruce, pp.226 f.; Lohse, p.93, n.1; compare *e.g.* 1 Cor. 11:2; 15:1-5; Phil. 4:9; 1 Thes. 4:1; 2 Thes. 3:6 – the latter pair also being closely joined with the idea of 'walking' in Christ's way.

related ideas occur elsewhere in this passage (see below). All this points to the probability that by 'receiving Christ Jesus as Lord' Paul here refers to the Colossian Christians' acceptance of the proclamation of Jesus the Lord, to their consequent confession of faith, and to their new status as members of Christ's body (see 2:19). All of these became theirs when (greatly daring in their pagan context) they took their stand of faith and submitted to Christian initiation.

Those who have (in this technical sense) 'received Christ Jesus as Lord' must *continue to live in him*: NIV thus brings out well the continuous force of the present imperative. The English word 'live' is ambiguous: it could mean life itself or ethical behaviour. Here, however, Paul's meaning is clear. Literally, the word means 'walk', which, in Jewish thought (see on 1:10, above) was and is the standard term for ethical conduct. Here the emphasis is on the sort of conduct *appropriate* for one who claims Jesus as Lord. This, the ultimate goal of Paul's argument, will be spelt out (3:1 – 4:6) after he has warned against a road which turns out to be a blind alley.

The new sort of behaviour has become a possibility for those who, having received Christ Jesus as Lord, are *rooted and built up in him, strengthened in the faith as you were taught, and overflowing with thankfulness*. How many of these metaphors were still 'live' for Paul it is hard to say. Even he must have had difficulty imagining Christians 'walking' in Christ by being well rooted like a tree, solidly built like a house, confirmed and settled like a legal document, and overflowing like a jug full of wine. Each of the images, nevertheless, has its own point to make. It is particularly worth noting that, whereas 'rooted' is an aorist, indicating a once-for-all planting of the Christian 'in' Christ, 'built up' is in the present, suggesting continual growth – an important theme in this letter to a very young church. It is grammatically uncertain whether, by 'strengthened in the faith', Paul means that their faith should itself become stronger, or that they should become stronger (in other respects) *by means of* their faith, or that they should become stronger in their grasp of 'the faith', *i.e.* Christianity as a whole. Paul could have said any of these: the immediate reference to the teaching they had received indicates that the last is probably correct. Thankfulness, filling the church so full that it constantly spills over, is placed in this letter at the centre of Christian living (see 1:12ff.; 3:15, 17; 4:2). As we saw above, gratitude to God is to be the main characteristic of God's people, 'a sign that they are indeed living in the new age'.[1] The church that learns truly to worship God is a church growing to full maturity. Paul has already given the Colossians plenty of reasons why they should thank God, and will shortly give them still more.

B. LET NO-ONE EXCLUDE YOU (2:8–23)

As we saw, finding divisions within 2:6 – 4:6 is somewhat arbitrary. The warnings in the present section against false teaching continue until 2:23; but 2:20 – 3:4 forms a balanced bridge between these warnings and the ethical instruction of chapter 3. This section begins, characteristically, with a summary statement (v.8), whose implications are then worked out. Its main thrust could be summarized as follows. The Colossians already possess all they need, through belonging to the crucified and risen Jesus Christ. Judaism, apparently offering so much to pagans, is itself just another form of the religious life of the 'present age', which has been superseded now that the Messiah has been raised from the dead and so has inaugurated 'the age to come'.

i. *Already complete in Christ* (2:8–15)

a. Christ and his rivals (2:8–10). **8.** Paul now sums up his negative advice to the Colossians: *See to it that no-one takes you captive.* The verb here translated 'take captive' (*sylagōgein*) is a very rare one. I suggest that Paul uses it because it makes a contemptuous pun with the word *synagogue*: see to it that no-one snatches you as a prey (see RSV) from the flock of Christ, to lock you up instead within Judaism. The means by which young Christians might be snatched away is characterized as

---

[1]Bruce, p.227. See the fine passage on grace and gratitude in K. Barth, *Church Dogmatics* vol. 4 (Eng. Tr.: T. and T. Clark, 1956), part 1, pp.41 ff.

through hollow and deceptive philosophy. NIV well expresses the fact that Paul is not opposed to (what we would call) 'philosophy' in general:[1] literally the word simply means 'love of wisdom'. But this 'love of wisdom', like the façade of a grand house which remains standing when the insides have been demolished, promises much and gives nothing. Hellenistic Judaism called itself a 'philosophy' on occasion, especially when in contact with the pagan world that thought in terms of competing philosophical schools.[2] Paul, referring to it thus, contemptuously agrees that it should be seen as just another human system.

In place of the treasures of wisdom and knowledge that the Colossians already possess in Christ (2:3), this 'philosophy' offers only *human tradition and the basic principles of this world.* 'Human tradition', a phrase picked up in 2:22, recalls the polemic of both Isaiah (29:13) and Jesus (Mk. 7:5ff.) against the transformation of true, living religion into a set of ideas and rules handed on at a purely human level. This is not to deny that there is a proper use of 'tradition' within Christianity, when Christ himself works by his Spirit to bring his truth to a new generation through the witness of the church. What Paul has in mind is undoubtedly the traditions of the Rabbinic schools in which he had grown up.

The second phrase, translated here as 'the basic principles of this world', is somewhat harder, though very important to the whole argument. The problem lies in the ambiguity of the word translated as 'basic principles' (*stoicheia*). NIV has opted for the meaning 'rudiments', the foundation principles of a subject: but the word could equally well mean the 'elements' supposed by early science to make up the physical world (earth, air, water and fire), or – as most scholars take it – the elemental spirits of the universe, identified as the 'deities' who preside over individual nations and peoples. All these meanings derive from the word's root meaning of 'series' or 'row' and hence 'member in a series', 'component' or (in that sense) 'element'. The context of Colossians 2 shows that here and in verse 20 the correct

[1] It has taken the 'and' in the phrase 'through philosophy and empty deceit' as epexegetic, so that instead of letting 'philosophy' stand by itself ('philosophy *and* hollow deception') it is modified by the second phrase (' "philosophy", *i.e.* hollow deception').

[2] See Introduction, p.26, and n.4.

meaning is that of local presiding deities, the national 'gods' supposed to rule over the different areas and races of the world. The arguments for this are well summarized by Caird,[1] and will be strengthened by our exegesis of this whole chapter.

But did Paul think that these presiding deities really 'existed'? His clearest answer is in 1 Corinthians 8:4–6.

> We know that an idol is nothing at all in the world and that there is no God but one. For even if there are so-called gods, whether in heaven or on earth (as indeed there are many 'gods' and many 'lords'), yet for us there is but one God . . . and but one Lord.

The gods may have some odd sort of existence, but they are not God. Certainly they 'existed' in the sense that pagans believed in them and worshipped them: Artemis (Diana), the great goddess of Ephesus, had better be taken seriously by anyone preaching the gospel in that city (cf. Acts 19:28–40). Three points are basic to Paul's argument about these 'powers'. (a) Christ is the ruler of all nations, and of any powers or authorities that may stand behind them in the shadowy world of superstition and mythology. (b) The Colossians, in being set free from their national solidarities by belonging to the new world-wide people of God, have also been released from their local 'deities'. (c) What Judaism might offer to ex-pagan Christians is in fact just another local and, one might say, tribal religion, composed like any other of allegiances, rules and regulations which function at a purely worldly level.[2]

The alternative to this superficially attractive 'philosophy' is the system of life and truth that depends on Christ: and with this the battle is joined. This passage brings to a climax the Christological theme that has been developing since 1:15–20, exploring one facet after another of what it means for Christians to be 'in' him (note the succession of 'in Christ' and

---

[1]Caird, p.190; see too his *Principalities and Powers*.
[2]The line of thought is therefore very close to Gal. 4:1–11.

similar phrases throughout 2:9ff.).

9–10. These verses give the main reason (*for*) why the Colossians must not be ensnared by this 'philosophy': *in Christ all the fulness of the Deity lives in bodily form.* This is probably to be taken simply as an expansion of 1:19; the tense is past there, present here, but in both the referent is the same, the glorified man Christ Jesus. The word translated 'in bodily form' can also mean 'actually' or 'in solid reality'.[1] We should not, however, drive a wedge between the two. Part of Paul's point is that the incarnation, the taking of 'bodily' form by God, was and is the 'solid reality' in which were fulfilled all the earlier foreshadowings, all the ancient promises that God would dwell with his people. The word *theotēs*, translated 'the Deity', is to be distinguished from *theiotēs*, 'divinity' – an attribute which might conceivably be possessed by a being of lesser standing than God himself. The verse is, of course, much more than a mere detached statement of a doctrine. It enables Paul to do two things. First, he shows that Christians have no need to pay homage to lesser supernatural beings: or, to put it more strongly, that all other lords become idols when contrasted with Christ. The man Jesus Christ, now exalted, is not one of a hierarchy of intermediary beings, angelic or (in some sense) 'divine'. He is, uniquely, 'God's presence and his very self'. Second, Paul is anxious to show that all the advantages of monotheism (which attracted many Gentiles by its contrast to the confused and unedifying pagan pantheon) accrue to Christianity. Christ is not a second, different Deity: he is the embodiment and full expression of the one God of Abraham, Isaac and Jacob.

Those who belong to him, therefore, *have been given fulness in Christ.* (The same root underlies both this phrase and 'all the fulness' in v.9.) The parallels in Ephesians (1:23; 3:19) suggest the meaning that God intends to flood the lives of men and women, and ultimately the whole creation, with his own love, power and richness, and that he has already begun to put this plan into effect through Christ and by his Spirit. That is the

---

[1]So Caird, pp.191 f., citing 2:17 as a parallel for the contrast of 'solid reality' with its 'shadowy' anticipations. This is fair enough: but his objections to 'in bodily form' can be met, along similar lines to the argument advanced above on 1:15.

Colossians' inheritance in Christ, and they can want nothing more from any other source. Nor need they submit to any other master, for *(he) is the head over every power and authority.* NIV, by translating 'head of . . .' as 'head over . . .', rightly indicates that 'head' here is not to be understood in terms of the 'head-and-body' metaphor of 1:18 and 2:19. The word 'head' was as flexible and evocative in Hebrew or Greek as it is in English, and we should not squeeze all Paul's uses of it into exactly the same mould. It is probable that 'every power and authority' here, and in verse 15, refers primarily to the same entities as the *stoicheia* of verse 8 (and perhaps the list of 'powers' in 1:16). They, at least, are the powers and authorities which are relevant to Paul's argument at this point.[1] All power structures, ancient or modern, whether political, economic or racial, have the potential to become rivals to Christ, beckoning his followers to submit themselves to them in order to find a fuller security. The invitation is as blasphemous as it is unnecessary. Christ brooks no rivals. His people need no-one but him.

b. Already circumcised in Christ (2:11-12). **11-12.** *In him you were also circumcised*: or, perhaps better, 'and in him you were circumcised'. Paul emphasizes that the Colossians have *already* been 'circumcised' (in a sense to be explained), and therefore do not need to undergo the operation again in a physical sense, as would be required if they were to become proselytes to Judaism. The emphatic position of this statement in Paul's argument is one of the strongest reasons for seeing Judaism as his main target in the present chapter.[2] The metaphorical use of 'circumcision' (*not with a circumcision done by the hands of men*) has a long history in the Old Testament and subsequent Jewish writings.[3] Paul picks up this idea (that the heart, not merely the body, requires circumcision) and uses it to distinguish between Christianity and unredeemed Judaism, thereby designating the

---

[1] On the wider significance of the idea of 'principalities and powers', beyond the scope of the argument here, see the references in n.1, p.72, above.

[2] Against, *e.g.*, Schweizer, pp.140 ff., who has to explain this reference away as peripheral. Our view provides, of course, another close link between Colossians and Galatians.

[3] *E.g.* Lv. 26:41; Je. 6:10; and at Qumran 1QS 5:5, 1QpHab 11:13 (Vermes, pp.78, 242). Paul also uses the idea in Rom. 2:29; Phil. 3:3.

former as the true inheritor of the promises to the patriarchs. 'Christian circumcision', the point of entry into the community of Christ's people (as physical circumcision was the point of entry into the community of Israel), provides all the initiation one needs to belong to the people of God.

But in what does this 'Christian circumcision' consist? Literally translated, this passage reads 'and in him you were circumcised with a circumcison not made with hands, in the stripping off of the body of the flesh, in the circumcision of Christ, having been buried with him in baptism . . .'. NIV has changed the order and opted for one of the possible interpretations of 'the circumcision of Christ', reading *you were also circumcised, in the putting off of the sinful nature* (the margin notes that this could be translated 'flesh'), *not with a circumcision done by the hands of men but with the circumcision done by Christ, having been buried with him in baptism* . . . This last phrase, which envisages Christ as the actual performer of the spiritual circumcision, is somewhat strained: better, perhaps, to leave the reference general, 'the circumcision relating to Christ', or 'circumcision as (re)defined by Christ', hence simply 'the Christian circumcision'.

The earlier phrase explaining this spiritual surgery ('the putting off of the sinful nature') is more tricky still. NIV omits the word 'body' (see the literal translation above): but, even if we reinstate it, the problem of meaning remains. In what sense does one 'strip off the body of flesh' in becoming a Christian? The NIV (and NEB) apparently resolve the problem in one direction by interpreting 'body of flesh' to mean 'sinful nature': the old Adam, as in Romans 6:2–6, is put to death in baptism. But 'stripping off the body of flesh', even allowing for the multiple meanings of 'flesh' in Paul, seems a very odd way of making this point. Some scholars have therefore suggested that the reference is to Christ's stripping off of his own flesh, in his death (this would imply that the final phrase, 'the circumcision of Christ', was a reference not to 'Christian circumcision' but to the death of Christ, metaphorically referred to as 'circumcision'). It is true that Paul understands the death of Jesus itself, and not merely the believer's appropriation of it for himself, as the moment when sins were dealt with (see, *e.g.*, 2:13–15 below).

But this is not the point here:[1] the context requires that Paul say something about what has happened to the Colossians in their becoming Christians. We must therefore enquire further.

One possible meaning of the words, the literal stripping off of the physical body, leaving (presumably) a naked soul or spirit, is obviously irrelevant to those who have yet to face physical death, and is scarcely Christian in its theology. A better solution might be to treat the phrase as meaning more or less the same as 3:9; but this reads into our present passage an unwarranted ethical emphasis. There is, however, another possible meta-phorical meaning which gives excellent sense here. As a result of their baptism into Christ, the Colossians now belong first and foremost to the family of God, and not, therefore, to the human families (and their local 'rulers') to which they formerly belonged. 'Body' can, in fact, easily carry the connotation of a group of people, needing further redefinition to make it clear which group is envisaged (as in 'body of Christ'). In that context 'flesh' can easily provide the further requisite definition, since it can carry not only the meanings of 'sinful human nature' but also, simultaneously, the meanings of *family* solidarity.[2] The phrase can thus easily mean 'in the stripping off of the old human solidarities'. The convert, in stripping off his clothes for baptism (the baptismal reference in the next verse has coloured the language) leaves behind, as every adult candidate for baptism in (say) a Muslim or Hindu society knows, the solidarities of the old life, the network of family and society to which, until then, he or she has given primary allegiance. This meaning fits very well with the rest of the section.

The transfer from the old solidarity to the new is accomplished in baptism. Such a statement alarms many Christians today: seeing the dangers of regarding baptism as a quasi-magical rite through which people are automatically trans-formed, many have drawn back from the realism of Paul's language, not only in this passage but in (for instance) Romans 6:2–11 and Galatians 3:27. It has sometimes been claimed either that 'baptism' here is simply a metaphor whose reference is the

---

[1] For other objections to this interpretation, see Caird, pp.193 f.
[2] See Rom. 11:14, where the Greek for 'my own people' is, literally, 'my flesh'.

'spiritual' event of becoming a Christian, or that the baptism in question has as its main significance the public profession of faith.

But Paul's thought is not to be forced into the 'either-or' of anachronistic Protestant – or, for that matter, Catholic – polemics. Paul is certainly not asserting anything remotely like the position Protestants have always rightly opposed, namely, that the rite of water-baptism 'makes someone a Christian' in the sense that the candidate is willy-nilly converted and made, automatically and inalienably, the possessor of eternal life. But his thought here contains another element. As a Jew, Paul had believed in the solidarity of the racial people of God. In becoming a Christian, he transferred to the church the idea that the people of God was indeed a *people* – not now, indeed, drawn from one race only, but made up from every family under heaven.[1] This people is not merely an invisible family known to God alone, but is an actual company of people in space and time, the church in which Christ is confessed as Lord: outward and visible entry into this outward and visible family is accomplished through the rite of baptism.

This explains Paul's frequent appeal that the church should become in fact what it is in theory, should put into detailed operation the life to which it has been committed in baptism. 1 Corinthians 10 shows that it is possible, in Paul's mind, for people to be baptized and yet to be in danger of losing all. This does not make baptism a mere empty ritual. The candidate, being placed into the family where Christ is loved and served, is in the best possible position to grow into mature Christian faith and life. If we find Paul's definite statements about the effects of baptism hard to understand, it is probably because we have lost his vision of the church as the loving and welcoming family of God, the people who, by support, example and teaching, enable one another to accept the gospel down to the depths of their being, and so to make real for themselves (among other things) the rich statements of Colossians 2:12, to which we now return.

Having been buried with him in baptism, so that his death is counted as their death, the Colossians have been – also in

---

[1]One of the clearest expressions of this whole position is Gal. 3:26-29.

baptism[1] – *raised with him through your faith.* Just as the doorway of a building will often indicate what sort of a building it is, so baptism, the gateway to the Christian life, demonstrates (compare Rom. 6:2–11) that being a Christian means dying with Christ to the old solidarities and habits and coming alive to the new family of God and its new life-style. Faith itself is the first sign of this spiritual life: not that spiritual life is God's reward for those who believe the gospel, but that true faith, expressed classically in the confession that Jesus is Lord, is the result of the secret life-giving work of God's own Spirit (see 1 Cor. 12:3).

As in Romans 4:16–25, this faith is characterized not simply as 'faith in Jesus Christ', but as *faith in the power of God, who raised him from the dead.* To believe that God raised Jesus from the dead[2] *is* to believe in the God who raises the dead. Such faith not merely assents to a fact about Jesus, it recognizes a truth about God. Paul, reminding the Colossians that they have professed this faith, draws attention to that characteristic of God which undergirds their new status in Christ. They belong to the new world, where the 'rulers' of the old world have no authority. By the same power that raised Jesus from the dead, the Colossians have been transferred (see 1:13) into the family of the new age. This does not mean (as is sometimes suggested) that, according to this passage, Christians live entirely in the new age – an idea which comes under attack in (*e.g.*) 1 Corinthians 4:8 or 2 Timothy 2:18. The 'heavenly' life which Christians now enjoy does not escape the rigours and temptations of earthly existence, but becomes on the contrary more than ever committed to working out the meaning of Christ's death and resurrection in practical human life (see 3:1–4; 3:5 – 4:6).[3]

c. *Already free from the law's demands* (2:13–15). It is utterly characteristic of Pauline theology that at the heart of a description of how people (particularly Gentiles) have come to belong to God's family we should find the cross. It is also characteristic

---

[1] NIV omits the repeated 'in which'.
[2] This is the second half (after 'Jesus is Lord') of the basic Christian confession, according to Rom. 10:9–10.
[3] See Caird, p.194; A. T. Lincoln, *Paradise Now and Not Yet: Studies in the Role of the Heavenly Dimension in Paul's Thought with Special Reference to his Eschatology* (CUP, 1981), ch. 5.

that Paul should see the power of the law as abolished in Christ's death, and that this thought should follow a similar statement about circumcision (see Rom. 4:9–12, 13–16). (It has been argued above, and will be borne out in the detailed exegesis, that the subject here is the Jewish law even though the word 'law' does not occur.[1]) That Colossians 2:13–15 provides a composite statement of this sort is not in question; but almost everything else about these verses is. In the case of many of the verbs here it is not even clear who the subject is, and the imagery employed seems to pile one obscurity on top of another. The context, however, indicates the overall line of thought. Paul is drawing out the significance of the fact that the new Christians have been united in baptism with the death and resurrection of Christ, and so have exchanged their previous status (Gentiles, outside the people of God) for that of forgiven sinners, welcomed into a family circle beyond the reach of legal accusation or previous national loyalties.

13. Every Jew would have agreed with Paul in telling the Colossians that, in their pagan days, *'you were dead in your sins and in the uncircumcision of your flesh'*.[2] The best commentary on this is provided by the parallel passage in Ephesians 2:12: 'remember that at that time you were separate from Christ, excluded from citizenship in Israel and foreigners to the covenants of the promise, without hope and without God in the world.' Paul nowhere draws back from the position that he would have taken as a Pharisee, that the pagan nations were utterly lost. Rather, he offers the appropriate remedy for this condition. Just as the Prodigal Son in Luke 15:24, 32 'was dead and is alive again', so *God made you[3] alive with Christ*. The verb in this sentence, formed by adding the word 'with' to 'made alive', is typical of expressions Paul uses when thinking about Christians dying and rising (or whatever) 'with Christ'.[4] The logic of

---

[1]See pp.24 ff., above.

[2]This follows NIV margin: the text gives 'your sinful nature'. This can hardly be correct. Their 'sinful nature' may have been, in a metaphorical sense, 'uncircumcised', but the word *sarx*, 'flesh', which Paul uses here, clearly indicates that as Gentiles they were literally and physically uncircumcised.

[3]Not 'us', as in margin: see below.

[4]*Cf.* Rom. 8:17; 2 Cor. 7:3; Eph. 2:6; Col. 3:1; 2 Tim. 2:11.

such constructions is that, when God looks at those who are 'in' Christ, he reckons that what is true of Christ (particularly his death and resurrection) is true of them also. They died *with* Christ, they have been raised *with* him. Events like resurrection, which were expected by Jews to occur at the end of time, have actually begun within history, so that those who belong to Christ find themselves living simultaneously in the old and in the new age, albeit owing fundamental allegiance to the new. It is this overlap of the two 'ages' of Jewish expectation that brings about the characteristic paradoxes and tensions of Paul's view of the Christian life. At one moment he must emphasize, as here, that believers already partake in the life and power of Christ's resurrection. At another (*e.g.* 3:5–11; Rom. 8:12–15) he must stress the consequent obligation to 'put to death' all that still remains of the old sinful life.

Because of the close biblical link between sin and death, the logical precondition for the resurrection life is that sins must be dealt with. The claim that God[1] has 'made you alive' requires, therefore, further explanation: and Paul answers this need, preliminarily, by saying that God *forgave us all our sins*. (The word 'all' goes with 'sins', not with 'us'.) Paul has altered his pronouns here: he has now shifted from 'you' to 'we'. Jews were not 'dead in physical uncircumcision', but they, just as much as pagans, needed forgiveness of sins. The Colossians have joined Paul in the people of God; Paul joins them in the category of forgiven sinners. The further question, of how this forgiveness was accomplished, is now to be addressed.

14. How, then, did the cross solve the problem of sin? Paul does not attempt here a full theological statement of the achievement of Calvary. He aims, more specifically, to show how those things that might have excluded the Colossians from God's people were dealt with on the cross. The present passage stands at the centre-point, both in literary structure and theology, of the whole chapter and section.

In verses 14–15 Paul notes the two barriers which stand between human beings and membership in God's family: *the*

---

[1]Unexpressed in the Greek, rightly supplied by NIV.

written code, with its regulations, that was against us and that stood opposed to us, on the one hand, and *the powers and authorities* on the other. God has apparently *cancelled* the former and *disarmed* the latter. But what are these two? And in what way were they 'against us'? And how has this antagonism been removed? Paul clearly intends to provide answers to all of these questions, but he has done so in a way that makes it difficult for us to hear what he has said. In verse 14 we must ask: (a) what is the 'written code'? (b) How does 'with its regulations' relate to the rest of the verse? (c) What does 'that stood opposed to us' add which was not already said in 'that was against us'? And, most important, (d) how has God 'cancelled' and 'taken away' this barrier? (The further problems of v.15 will be discussed presently.) NIV, like all translations, has had to opt for one particular point of view, and has in consequence made the passage seem simpler than it is.

We may begin by looking at (a) and (b) together. There are basically three options for understanding *cheirographon* (a word that occurs only rarely in literature of this time). (i) The first is taken by NIV, which, translating it as 'the written code', and linking it to 'with its regulations' (*tois dogmasin*) (cf. 2:20), sees it as referring to the Mosaic law. This can claim a parallel in Ephesians 2:15, the only other Pauline use of the root *dogma*. (ii) The more traditional interpretation was to understand *cheirographon* as a bond of debt, an IOU, signed by the debtor,[1] referring in this case metaphorically to the debt of sin. This can be coupled with a view of 'its regulations' which takes it with one of the two phrases indicating that this bond was 'against us' ('against us' *because of* its regulations: there is no word for 'with' in the Greek, and the dative case here employed could be interpreted like this). There are grammatical difficulties with this, though, as indeed there appear to be in doing almost anything with the phrase except, like Chrysostom and one fourteenth-century manuscript, omitting it altogether.[2] (iii) A

---

[1]Reference is sometimes made here to Phm. 19, on which see the commentary.

[2]Another, equally implausible, suggestion is that the passage embodies a pre-Pauline fragment which Paul has modified by the clumsy insertion of these words: see Lohse, pp.109 f., and Martin, 'Reconciliation and Forgiveness in Colossians', in *Reconciliation and*

recent interpretation draws on the use of *cheirographon* in a first-century Jewish apocalyptic work to refer to a book, kept by an angel, in which all one's evil deeds were recorded, and couples this with the suggestion that Paul sees Christ himself as taking on the identity of this bond, nailed to the cross, in representing his sinful people.[1]

The last suggestion seems to me forced and unlikely. If Paul really meant that Christ himself became the *cheirographon*, he would surely have made it clear sooner than at the end of the verse. And the idea of an IOU, while undoubtedly true to the usage of the word, has to import into the context the notion that this bond had been signed by all people in their consciences – which, while it may correspond to a truth about universal consciousness of guilt, reads a great deal of extraneous material into an already crowded verse. But options (ii) and (iii) may have a grain of truth in them, because they can in fact be combined with (i). It would be in keeping with the ironic tone we find at various points in this chapter that Paul should refer to the Mosaic Law as a mere IOU note, or perhaps as a book which does nothing but keep a tally of one's sins (see, *e.g.*, Rom. 4:15; 5:20; and Gal. 3:19–22, where the law, given by angels, has the purpose and effect of shutting people up in their sins). *Tois dogmasin* is then an almost equally ironic explanatory phrase, referring to the detailed commandments of the Law as that in which the 'handwritten note' consisted. The first alternative, properly understood, thus contains at least the overtones of the other two, neither of which is satisfactory if forced to bear the whole weight of meaning. If this suggestion is correct, the other problems in the verse may be seen in a new light.

(c) The difference between 'against us' and 'opposed to us' is slight but not altogether insignificant. The first indicates active opposition or enmity: the second, a barrier which stands in one's way. The word-order in Greek is 'having blotted out the against-us handwriting, with its regulations, which was opposed to us'. This may indicate that Paul added the last phrase to emphasize the effect of the detailed regulations,

---

Hope: New Testament Essays on Atonement and Eschatology Presented to L. L. Morris on his 60th Birthday, ed. R. Banks (Eerdmans, 1974), pp. 104–124, here at pp.117 ff.

[1]For the evidence, and references to discussions of it, see Martin, pp.83–86.

because of which the 'handwriting' – *i.e.* the Law – kept both Jews and Gentiles locked up in sin. The Mosaic Torah did not, we should note, stand over against Jews and Gentiles in the same way. In Paul's view, it shut *up* the Jews under sin and shut *out* the Gentiles from the hope and promise of membership in God's people.

(d) God not only 'cancelled'[1] this 'written code'; he *took it away*, (by) *nailing it to the cross*. The images are so overlaid here that it is hard to see how they are to be related to each other. But if we follow the line of thought taken so far, and pick up the suggestion of several writers[2] that there is a reference back to the *titulus*, 'The King of the Jews', which Pilate nailed to the cross as the ostensible reason for Jesus' execution (see Jn. 19:19), the following interpretation suggests itself. Jesus was sent to the Roman tribunal after being deemed worthy of death by a Jewish court, which had declared (whatever we make of the details) that he was guilty according to the law. Pilate, echoing that verdict but giving it a new twist, put on the cross the sign that read 'The King of the Jews'. But Paul, looking at the cross, saw there instead the *titulus* that expressed the charge against all Jesus' people, the written code that stood over against them, disqualifying them from the life of the new age. And it was God, not Pilate, who put it there. Underneath the different emphases required by the different arguments in which they are set, this verse states the same truth as Galatians 3:13 or 2 Corinthians 5:21. As the representative of his people, Jesus dies their death on the cross, so that, dying it with him, they need never die again. This is how God has dealt with sin, so that his people may have new life.

The context safeguards this statement of what Luther called the 'wondrous exchange' (Christ takes our sins, we his righteousness, as in 2 Cor. 5:21) against the misunderstandings to which it has sometimes been subjected. God himself is the source of the redeeming action, not at all an unwilling angry tyrant, pacified by his Son's pleading or, worse, by the sight of blood. And Christ dies under the 'written code' that stood

---

[1]Literally 'has wiped out' or 'has blotted out'; with ancient inks the papyrus could actually be washed clean (see Williams, pp.96 f.).

[2]*E.g.* Dibelius-Greeven; my interpretation here is quite close to that of Caird, p.195.

against us (the second 'us' may be emphatic, in implied contrast with Christ who took it in our place) not in virtue of some arbitrary exchange of roles but because he, as Messiah, truly represents his people and can therefore appropriately stand in their place.

This verse, understood in this fashion, does two things in its wider context. First, it explains how God has made forgiveness of sins, and therefore new life, available for all. Second, it re-emphasizes the uselessness of looking to Judaism for a richer or more complete membership in the people of God. The Torah was not a help, but a hindrance; God has erased its accusing demands and removed them from the scene altogether. No longer need Jews be under its curse; no longer can it keep Gentiles out of God's family. No longer can it bar the way to the life of the age to come. This emphasis, reinforced by the final verse (15) of the present section, is taken up again in the last sections of the chapter (2:16–19, 20–23).

15. The overall point of verse 15 is likewise clear, but the details are once more extremely tricky to unravel. Paul is asserting that, because of what Jesus did on the cross, *the powers and authorities* are a beaten, defeated lot, so that (by implication) neither the Colossians nor anyone else who belongs to Jesus need be overawed by them again. The phrase *triumphing over them* alludes metaphorically to the practice of Roman generals following a conquest. In the days before the modern news media, the most spectacular method of announcing a far-off victory to people at home was to march in triumph through the city, displaying the booty taken from conquered peoples, and leading a host of bedraggled prisoners through the streets as *a public spectacle.*

So far, so good; but here the problems of this verse start. (a) What precisely has been done to the 'powers'? (b) By whom has it been done (God? or Christ?) and (c) where has it been done (in Christ? or on the cross?). These three questions need to be taken together. Logically and grammatically, the subject of the sentence continues to be 'God', and the final phrase, which could mean either 'in him' or 'in it' (*i.e.* the cross), would read more naturally as a reference to God's action 'in Christ'. (Compare 'with him' two verses earlier.) Thus RSV: 'he disarmed the principalities and powers and made a public example of them, triumphing over them in him'. But the verb translated 'disarmed' by both RSV and NIV is in a form which elsewhere – in 3:9, for instance – refers to stripping something off from *oneself*.[1] This has led several writers to suggest a view composed of three elements, as follows: (i) Paul has subconsciously slipped into regarding Christ, not God, as the subject; (ii) the odd resultant idea of Christ's 'stripping off the powers and authorities' is to be explained by seeing them as the powers of evil which were using his physical body as their point of entry and attack, so that in divesting himself of his 'flesh' he got rid of that through which he was vulnerable;[2] (iii) the final phrase should not be understood as 'in Christ' but 'in the cross'.

Of these three elements, (i) and (iii) are quite possible. But about (ii) it must be said that, first, there is nothing in the passage which warrants understanding the 'powers' as (what we think of as) 'the powers of evil', identical with Satan and his angels; second, the mixture of metaphors in the verse would be very harsh, with Christ 'celebrating a triumph over a cast off suit of clothes' (Caird); and, third, the idea that the 'powers' had their point of entry in Christ's physical body, of which he therefore divested himself, is more gnostic than Pauline. It seems better therefore (despite the apparent parallel in 3:9) to take the verb in an active sense, which in Hellenistic Greek it could quite easily have,[3] and say that God, or possibly Christ, 'stripped' not himself, but the rulers and authorities.

It is still not obvious, however, why Paul should assert here that God has, in Christ, 'stripped' the rulers and authorities and held them up to contempt. But this may become clearer if we consider the verse within the passage as a whole.

I have suggested above that the *stoicheia* in 2:8, 20 and the 'powers and authorities' of 2:10, 15 refer primarily in this context

[1]See NEB: 'he discarded the cosmic powers and authorities like a garment'. This view finds some apparent support in 1 Cor. 2:6–8: but see below.

[2]See the first alternative in the NEB margin: 'he stripped himself of his physical body, and thereby boldly made a spectacle of the cosmic powers and authorities, and led them . . .': this view can be coupled with the interpretation of v.11 above, which sees in it a reference to Christ's own 'stripping off' – the same root word is used – of his flesh.

[3]See, *e.g.*, Lohse, pp.111 ff.

to the hypothetical tutelary 'gods' of the different nations. Among these nations Paul includes Israel, to whom God, through his angels, had given a national charter, the Law. The point he wishes to make is that the Colossians had formerly been under the domination of these powers, (a) because they were members of pagan society and its religions, and (b) because the angels who had given the Law thus functioned as guardians, keeping Gentiles excluded from the family of God (see vv. 16–19). They have now been freely welcomed into that family (vv. 11–12), and this has been achieved through Christ's overpowering of the gaolers that had kept them locked up (see Rom. 11:32; Gal. 3:22).

At this point there is, I suggest, a further note of heavy and striking irony. The 'rulers and authorities' of Rome and of Israel – as Caird points out, the best government and the highest religion the world of that time had ever known – conspired to place Jesus on the cross. These powers, angry at his challenge to their sovereignty, stripped *him* naked, held *him* up to public contempt, and celebrated a triumph over *him*. In one of his most dramatic statements of the paradox of the cross, and one moreover which shows in what physical detail Paul could envisage the horrible death that Jesus had died, he declares that, on the contrary, on the cross God was stripping *them* naked, was holding *them* up to public contempt, and leading *them* in his own triumphal procession – in Christ, the crucified Messiah. When the 'powers' had done their worst, crucifying the Lord of glory *incognito* on the charge of blasphemy and rebellion, they had overreached themselves.[1] He, neither blasphemer nor rebel, was in fact their rightful sovereign. They thereby exposed themselves for what they were – usurpers of the authority which was properly his. The cross therefore becomes the source of hope for all who had been held captive under their rule, enslaved in fear and mutual suspicion. Christ breaks the last hold that the 'powers' had over his people, by dying on their behalf. He now welcomes them into a new family in which the ways of the old world – its behaviour, its distinctions of race and class and sex, its blind obedience to the 'forces' of politics, economics, pre-

[1]See 1 Cor. 2:7–8; the whole context (1:18 – 2:16) contains several parallels to Colossians.

judice and superstition – have become quite simply out of date, a ragged and defeated rabble. Verse 15 thus draws out the effect of verse 14.[1]

This passage raises sharply the question: how can Paul, who said earlier that 'all things' were *reconciled* to God through the cross (1:19–20; see the commentary there), declare here that on the cross the powers have been *defeated*? The missing clue, unstated but understood, is the doctrine of the fall. When God looked at his creation, made in and for Christ (1:15–17), he knew it to be very good. As it stood it did not need 'reconciling'. The intervention of sin produced a triple estrangement – between God and humanity, humanity and the world (including estrangements between individuals and races), and (consequently) God and the world (see Rom. 8:19ff.). God's response to this situation was one of sovereign love. Wanting the very best for his world, he determined to rid it entirely of the evil which has corrupted it at its very heart. The cross is therefore, at the same time, *both* the affirmation of God's hatred of sin and its foul consequences (especially the defacing of his image in his human creatures) *and* the affirmation of his steadfast determination to save humanity and the world. The ambiguity between the 'defeat' of 2:15 and the 'reconciliation' of 1:19 is therefore analogous to the similar double truth of God's attitude towards sinful human beings. As sinners, they need to die to sin; as human beings made in God's image, they need to have their true humanity reaffirmed and recreated in the resurrection. This is what Paul will work out in 2:20 – 3:4.

Though the 'rulers and authorities', then, had come to embody the rebellion of the world, they are not evil in themselves. God has made his world in such a way that corporate human life at any level will structure itself and order its affairs in particular ways. Different parts of the natural order, however, (*e.g.* the sun or moon) can be, and often have been, idolized, so that human beings offer to them that worship which belongs to God alone (see Rom. 1:25), and thus wrongly give them power in the world. The same can be true of the 'power structures' of the different nations (*e.g.* the goddess Roma in the ancient

[1] This is brought out in JB by 'and so . . . .'

world, or, more recently, Britannia) or the 'laws' governing social or economic life (*e.g.* the profit motive). Such things, like the sun and moon, are in themselves part of the good creation. Even a secular or pagan state can be regarded as bringing God's intended order into the world of human affairs (Rom. 13:1ff.). If worshipped, however, they attain to the rank, and power, of idols.

In what way, then, are they 'reconciled' (1:18)? This is certainly not something that has been put into automatic effect at the time of the crucifixion. It remains a programme to be fulfilled: 'that in everything he might *become* pre-eminent' (1:18; see 1 Cor. 15:20–28). It is to be effected through the work, and proclamation, of the church (Eph. 3:10). The reconciling mission of the church in the world therefore includes the task of proclaiming to the present 'power structures' that God is God, that Jesus is Lord, and summoning them to climb down from his throne and take up their proper responsibilities in looking after his world. Having been defeated as rebels, they now can be reconciled as subjects. They do not own the world. They do not hold the keys of death and hell. They (the Law included), being essentially of 'this age', do not hold final authority over those who belong already to the 'age to come'.

ii. *Therefore, do not submit to Jewish regulations (2:16–23)*

a. These things were mere preparations for Christ's new age (2:16–19). As often with Paul, the most significant word is the connective – in this case the *Therefore* at the start of verse 16. Paul is drawing out the implications of the victory of Christ over the rulers and authorities. They had tried to disqualify Gentiles from membership in God's people, holding up 'the handwriting, with its regulations' as a barrier against them. Now Paul warns the Colossians against letting any ordinary mortal do what the 'powers' have failed to do.

16–17. The first of the two negative commands of this section is *do not let anyone judge you* – perhaps better, with RSV, 'pass judgment on you'. This is not so much a matter of someone criticizing them (J. B. Phillips), taking them to task (NEB) or deciding for them (JB). It is a matter of excluding them, or informing them that they are excluded, from the people of God, on the basis of the Law's regulations which, according to verse 14, no longer stand in their way. This, broadly speaking, was what had happened (or was threatening to happen) to the Christians in Galatia (see Gal. 4:17). The phrase *by what you eat or drink* refers to the kosher laws of the Old Testament, extended, as they already were in Paul's time, to include wine as well as food.[1] Or *with regard to a religious festival, a new moon celebration or a Sabbath day* is a fairly typical list of Jewish holy days (*e.g.* Ezk. 45:17; Ho. 2:11), referring in descending order to the great annual festivals, the monthly celebrations and the weekly Sabbaths. These rules of diet and ritual marked out the Jew from his pagan neighbour. Failure to observe them implied that one did not belong to God's people.

It is interesting to observe what Paul does *not* say in opposition. He never says, here or in Galatians, that Christianity has nothing to do with Judaism. That would have been an equally effective argument in urging the Colossians (or the Galatians) to have no truck with Jewish regulations; but it would have cut off the branch upon which his whole argument rests, namely, the belief that Christianity is the *fulfilment* of Judaism. Christians are members of the 'age to come' for which Israel had been waiting. But 'when the perfect is come, the partial is abolished' (1 Cor. 13:10): or, as he puts it here, *these are a shadow of the things that were to come; the reality, however, is found in Christ.*

This language of 'shadow and substance' could be used in Hellenistic Greek in a Platonic sense, contrasting the 'shadowy' world of material objects with the 'real' world of 'forms' or of spiritual realities. It is true that Paul appears to be drawing up a contrast here between outward material regulations and inward spiritual truths.[2] But, just as he never says that Christianity has

---

[1] Perhaps by extension of the Nazirite rules in, *e.g.*, Nu. 6:3, or by the wider application of rules for priests ministering in the tabernacle, Lv. 10:9. See too the rule forbidding the seething of a kid in its mother's milk (Ex. 23:19; 34:26; Dt. 14:21), which was extended by Rabbinic interpretation to the prohibition of drinking any milk with any meat (Mishnah, *Hullin*, 8:1 ff.: see H. Danby *The Mishnah, Translated from the Hebrew with Introduction and Brief Explanatory Notes* (OUP, 1933), pp.524 f.).

[2] Compare the heading in J. B. Phillips' translation at this point: 'It is the spiritual, not the material, attitude which matters.'

nothing to do with Judaism, so he never says that it has nothing to do with material things, even with outward forms of worship and ritual. There are, in fact, four reasons why verse 17 should not be understood as a polemic against 'material' things *per se*.

First, Christianity, too, is a world-affirming religion, with its own outward symbols (see 2:12, *etc.*), intended to be lived out in concrete reality (3:5ff.). To 'demythologize' verse 16 into a condemnation of all outward regulations is to fall into a kind of modern gnosticism or antinomianism.

Second, verse 18 objects equally strongly to a *non*-material feature of the teaching to which Paul is objecting, which would have slipped through the net were he simply attacking outward regulations.

Third, and most important, the phrase 'of the things that were to come', which qualifies 'shadow', shows that the proper contrast is that between the old age and the new. Christ has inaugurated the 'age to come'. The regulations of Judaism were designed for the period when the people of God consisted of one racial, cultural and geographical unit, and are simply put out of date now that this people is becoming a world-wide family. They were the 'shadows' that the approaching new age casts before it. Now that the reality is come, there is no point in clinging to the shadows. And the reality belongs to Christ.[1]

Fourth, there is a good reason why Paul would have used just this language to make his point. His style of argument throughout this passage is heavily ironic, portraying Judaism as 'another religion' in order to show that Christians do not need it for completeness. Here he is in effect saying: even in terms of pagan religion itself, Judaism has to do with the shadow-world, not with reality. The word for 'reality' here is *sōma*, which elsewhere regularly means 'body': so that the phrase could be translated 'the body of Christ'. Since this seems quite out of keeping with the context, *sōma* is usually taken solely as the opposite of *skia*,

---

[1]See RSV 'belongs to Christ'; NEB 'the solid reality is Christ's'. NIV 'found in Christ' is an attempt to catch the significance of the rather odd phrase 'the reality of Christ', which lacks any verb. Perhaps the genitive is really a defining one (see Moule, *Idiom Book*, pp.37 ff.): 'the reality *consists in* Christ'; and perhaps this way of putting it is suggested to Paul by the parallel between the nominative and genitive in each part of the verse ('a shadow of the coming things: the substance of Christ').

shadow, and this meaning is undoubtedly the primary one. But the proximity, within the same argument, of verse 19, where the 'head' and the 'body' are introduced quite casually, may suggest that Paul is aware of, and wishes to exploit, a *double entendre* here. He manages to refer at the same time to the substantiality of the new people of God, as opposed to the shadowy nature of the old, and to the fact that this new people is the 'body of Christ'.

18. If the target of verse 16 was a self-appointed judge, here it is a self-appointed umpire, who might declare that the Colossians were not playing the game according to the rules: *Do not let anyone . . . disqualify you for the prize.* This metaphor restates Paul's basic appeal: you are already members of the body of Christ, and nobody must be allowed to rule you out of court. This time the potential objection is based, not on non-observance of Jewish diet or festivals, but on their failure to share in a particular style of 'spiritual' life or mystical experience. The adverse ruling might come from one *who delights in*[1] *false humility and the worship of angels.* The word translated 'false humility' carries a bad connotation only by its place in the argument (here and in v.23): in 3:12 the same word is part of the description of Christian character. It may be that it should be linked more closely with the following phrase: compare JB, 'people who like grovelling to angels and worshipping them'. The word is used in some Jewish writings almost as a synonym for the fasting which in some disciplines was believed to induce heavenly visions.

This, however, points us on to the question: were the people Paul is attacking actually worshipping angels, and if so what sort of religion or philosophy did they think they were practising? To this there are three main lines of reply. The first searches through the various known syncretistic movements of the period for signs of worship explicitly offered to angels, and comes up with a variety of possible answers, none of them very satisfactory as a background for the chapter as a whole. The

---

[1]The Greek here – a strange semitic-sounding phrase (*thelōn en*) – is without parallel in the New Testament.

second takes 'the worship of angels' in the sense, not of human beings worshipping angels, but of the worship the angels themselves offer to God, and refers to various texts from post-biblical Judaism, not least Qumran, in which such a human participation in the angelic liturgy is attempted and advocated. The third takes the phrase in the same sense as the first, but sees it as another example of Paul's heavy irony: the people he is opposing spend so much time in speculations about angels, or in celebrating the fact that the law was given by them, that they are in effect worshipping them instead of God – a charge which the Jews of Paul's day would no doubt have rejected indignantly, but which it might have been difficult for them to refute.[1]

This third view fits the tone and context of Colossians 2 very well. The point about participation in angelic liturgies is well taken, but could simply be part of the reason for Paul's contemptuous reference here to a worship which, while apparently heavenly-minded and super-spiritual, was in fact bordering on idolatry.[2]

Paul has three different things to say about a person who insists on this kind of 'spirituality'. The third one, that such a person is out of touch with the Head, we shall come to presently. In the second, that *his unspiritual mind puffs him up with idle notions*, Paul drags the false worship back down to earth where it belongs. For the 'super-spirituality' of which such teachers boasted Paul substitutes 'unspirituality' (literally 'the mind of the flesh'). The phrase 'with idle notions' translates a single word in the Greek, which could mean 'without cause', *i.e.* nothing is achieved by this self-inflation. Though it could belong grammatically with the other adjacent phrase, 'Such a person . . . what he has seen' (see below), it seems better to take it where NIV has it. This warning against confusing the supernatural with the genuinely 'spiritual' remains relevant throughout the history of religion; it is perhaps particularly pertinent to Christians living in a rationalistic age, who may be tempted to regard a wide variety of paranormal or supernatural occurrences

[1]Caird (p.199) suggests a variation on this idea: obedience to the Torah is really worship offered to the angels who gave it. On the whole question see Introduction, pp.23 ff.
[2]See Caird, p.199; Houlden, p.197.

as somehow 'spiritual'.[1]

But the first accusation in this sequence of three almost defies translation, let alone comprehension. NIV, rendering *Such a person goes into great detail about what he has seen*, preserves the basic meaning of 'entering' which is inherent in the verb, but does so only by the use of the English idiom 'goes into detail', a metaphor with a different meaning altogether. RSV gives up the attempt and renders 'taking his stand on visions': comprehensible, but the Greek simply does not say that. NEB, for once leading the field in sticking to the literal sense of the text, reads 'people who . . . try to enter into some vision of their own'; but the problem is to decide what that *means*. Many manuscripts, reflected in AV, read the word 'not', which betrays its secondary origin by giving a much easier sense: 'intruding into those things which he hath not seen'. If, as some have recently argued,[2] the word means 'enter' in the sense of entry into heavenly mysteries, then we are clearly still in the world of super-spirituality. Perhaps the best solution is, again, to detect irony: with an implied contrast to 'entry into the worship of heaven itself', Paul describes these people as 'entering into – their own visions!' All they have discovered in their vaunted mystical experiences is a set of imaginary fantasies.

19. Finally, such a teacher *has lost connection with the Head*. NIV has changed the verb from negative to positive, emphasizing the view that those who propagate the teaching Paul is opposing were Christians who had become misguided, or who had never really understood their faith in the first place. It is possible, however, that the verb should be read, ambiguously, as 'and not *holding on to* the head', leaving the question open whether they were simply Jews who, according to Paul, had never 'grasped' Christ in the first place (the verb can mean just that) and now find themselves like a torso without a head. This is in fact more likely (see Introduction, p.28). The picture of Christ as the head is derived, obviously, from that development of his earlier 'body of Christ' metaphor (1 Cor. 12, *etc.*) which

---

[1]This is an important emphasis in the commentary by R. C. Lucas.
[2]See F. O. Francis in *Conflict*, pp. 197–207, and the discussion in Schweizer, pp.160–162.

Paul has already used in 1:18. It is not to be identified with the related idea in 2:10, though it may perhaps be related to the last phrase of verse 17, on which see above. The underlying point of this short description of the church as Christ's body is that, while the false teaching might try to exclude the Colossians from membership in God's people, in reality it is they, not the Colossians, who are in danger of being excluded. The true test of whether or not one belongs to God's people is neither the observance of dietary laws and Jewish festivals, nor the cultivation of super-spiritual experiences, but whether one belongs to Christ, alive with his life.

The church, then, takes its life from Christ himself, *from whom the whole body, supported and held together by its ligaments and sinews, grows as God causes it to grow,* or, perhaps, as God *wants* it to grow (see NEB). Private visions isolate individuals; dietary laws isolated the Jewish nation from the rest of the world; but in God's plan all belong together in mutual interdependence. It is no shame when a Christian finds that he or she cannot grow spiritually without support and help from fellow-believers; it is, rather, a surprise that anyone should have thought such a thing possible, let alone desirable. Literally, the verse reads 'grows with growth of God': NIV rightly takes this to mean 'from God'. It may also indicate that the new life of Christians is God's own life, echoing the theme we observed in 1:6, 11, *etc.*

b. *With Christ you died to this world and its regulations* (2:20-23). Paul uses his final appeal against the false teaching as a gateway through which to pass, by contrast, to the positive teaching of chapter 3. The opening words of the two subsections (2:20, 'since you died with Christ'; 3:1, 'since . . . you have been raised with Christ') show the parallel between them, which is worked out in detail in the two appeals. It is not really helpful to divide Paul's thought here into 'doctrine' (chs. 1-2) and 'ethics' (chs. 3-4): a good deal of what he has already said has had to do with behaviour, and a good deal that is to come is substantially doctrinal. The string of imperatives in chapter 3[1] hardly proves

[1]3:1, 2, 5, 8, 9, 12, 15 (twice), 16, 17, 18, 19, 20, 21, 22, 23, (perhaps 24: see the commentary on that verse); 4:1, 2, 5. A good many of these have further dependent participles, imperative in intent.

that a transition has occurred, since the basic mood of 2:6–23 is also imperative.[1] In both sections the commands are undergirded with doctrinal teaching. Perhaps the doctrine/ethics distinction is not so much a feature of Paul's thought as the comparatively modern dichotomy, of which Paul would been innocent, between facts and values. While, then, 2:20–23 is a separate section, part of 2:8–23 as a whole, we should not overlook its intimate connection with 3:1ff.

20. This final appeal, like the earlier ones in the chapter, is grounded in that reality which is true of the Colossians because they belong to Christ (2:11ff.). Christ, by his death, came out from under the apparent dominion which the 'powers' had exercised over him. Those who are his have therefore already emerged from that old tyranny. This is expressed in the words *since* (literally 'if': but this is the 'if', not of doubt, but of logic) *you died with Christ to the basic principles of this world*. Death releases people from their previous status: the idea here is similar to Paul's expressions elsewhere about dying 'to the law'.[2] Here the 'death' which the Colossians have already undergone is 'out from under' (perhaps the most literal way of reading *apo*, more simply interpreted as 'to' in NIV, RSV) the rule of the 'principles' or 'elements', mentioned already in verse 8.

The 'elements' and their characteristic regulations are 'of the world': *why*, then, *as though you still belonged to it* (*i.e.* the world), *do you submit to its rules?* In the light of the whole passage, it would be better to translate the verb as passive, not middle, seeing the sentence not as a rebuke for a lapse but as a warning of danger ('why should you allow yourselves to be subjected to its rules?', *cf.* AV). The meaning of 'rules' is defined by its context. It is not a warning against just any regulations at all, as has sometimes been implied, but against those that 'belong to the world' – which carries with it the overtones of rebellion against God, much like 'the present evil age' (*cf.* Gal. 1:4) as opposed to 'the age to come'. At the same time, Paul is preparing for the point (to be spelt out in vv.21–22) that these

---

[1] *Cf.* 2:6, 8, 16, 18.
[2] Rom. 7:2, 4, 6; *cf.* Rom. 6:7; Gal. 2:19. This whole subsection, indeed, is close to Rom. 6:8–11 (so Williams, p.113).

regulations betray their irrelevance for true holiness by dealing with physical things only, instead of with physical things in their full context.

21. It hardly needs to be said that this verse is a contemptuous reference to the sort of regulations Paul is opposing, not a statement of his own views. NIV has, in fact, brought this out by putting quotation marks round the three prohibitions, and a question mark at the end of the verse. The verb here translated 'handle'[1] is stronger than that rendered 'touch', thus producing a downward sliding scale (*Do not handle! Do not taste! Do not touch!*) which corresponds to the upward rise in absurd scrupulosity. Examples of this sort of regulation are not difficult to find in the Judaism roughly contemporary with Paul. There is no reason either to look to pagan sources or to imagine that only when one has found a religion which said *exactly* what Paul here says has the correct background been located. The tone throughout the passage has been heavily ironic, and this continues to the end of the chapter.

22. The two arguments here advanced against regulations of this sort are so close to those found on the lips of Jesus in Matthew 15:1–20 and Mark 7:1–23[2] that many scholars have suggested a conscious echo on Paul's part. This may be judged probable whether or not the Colossians would have picked up such a reference. The first argument, *these are all destined to perish with use*, highlights the futility of regulations dealing with materials – *i.e.* foodstuffs – whose proper use is also their destruction (*cf.* 1 Cor. 6:13). 'Perish with use' does not just mean 'may wear out in time', but indicates that 'the things could not be used without rendering them unfit for further use'.[3] The second argument, *because they are based on human commands or teachings*, refers, like Matthew 15:9, to Isaiah 29:13, where the prophet condemns his contemporaries for their heartless out-

[1]Some, without very good evidence, have suggested that this 'command' might refer to the practice of abstaining from marriage (see the discussion in Schweizer, pp.166 f.): but the argument of v.22 would hardly work if the verb here were restricted to that meaning.
[2]See too Tit. 1:14.
[3]So Lightfoot, p.204. Compare JB, 'perish by their very use': AV, 'perish with the using'.

ward show of religion. NIV seems to imply, with its addition of 'because' to the Greek original, that this clause is supposed to be the reason why foodstuffs will perish with use, but this is clearly absurd. The two clauses stand in parallel, both commenting independently on the regulations mocked in verse 21.

23. The Greek of the last verse of chapter 2 is sufficiently odd for several sober-minded commentators to suggest that, despite the absence of manuscript variations, scribal corruption has occurred at an early stage in transmission. Against this it must be said that any manuscript which offered an easy way out of the problems of verse 23 would instantly become suspect for just that reason; scribes are more likely to smooth out oddities than to introduce them. The first half of the verse is not too difficult, though a little awkward in expression. NIV translates, probably rightly, *such regulations indeed have an appearance of* (possibly 'a reputation for') *wisdom, with their self-imposed worship* (the most likely meaning of a word which occurs only here: it could also indicate a self-imposed discipline heavily enforced), *their false humility* (as in v. 18, the idea 'false' has to be supplied from the context) *and their harsh treatment of the body.* It is not difficult to picture the sort of religion Paul is opposing here. Its elaborate liturgies and seemingly rigorous self-abasing asceticism give it a name for serious piety: but it is a sham.

Why it is a sham Paul apparently says in the second half of the verse. But what exactly his reason may be has long baffled commentators.[1] One suggested alternative (*e.g.* RSV margin) gives a strong charge against these regulations: they 'are of no value, serving only to indulge the flesh'. What looks like rigorous discipline is in fact a subtle form of self-indulgence. This involves reading most of the verse as a parenthesis: 'which are (though possessing a reputation for wisdom with their self-imposed worship, abject grovellings and harsh physical discipline, all to no value) merely a way of gratifying the flesh'. This may ease the grammatical problem in the first part of the verse, where the main verb 'are' (*estin*) is followed almost at once by an accusative participle 'having' (*echonta*), but at the cost of

[1]For a good discussion see Moule, pp.108 ff.

straining the rest of the sentence almost unbearably. Another alternative is to take the Greek word *timē* (here rendered 'value') in its more usual sense of 'honour', and to suggest that perhaps these practices do not give proper honour to the human body; but this imports too many extraneous ideas into the clause. It is safest overall to follow NIV (and RSV): *they (i.e.* these regulations) *lack any value in restraining sensual indulgence.* This takes the clause as a single whole, understanding *pros plēsmonēn tēs sarkos,* literally 'towards the gratifying of the flesh', as modifying *timē,* 'value'.[1] The value these practices do *not* have is precisely the one which might make them worth while, and which their supporters claim for them: that they restrain fleshly indulgence (which includes not only sensuality but also jealousy, anger and so forth: see Gal. 5:19–21). Genuine holiness, which is an anticipation of the life of the age to come into which the risen Christ has already entered (1:18; 3:1–4), is not to be had by methods whose very nature, focusing as it does on perishable material things, binds them to the present age.

C. INSTEAD, LIVE IN ACCORDANCE WITH THE NEW AGE (3:1 – 4:6)

How, then, is genuine holiness to be had? Paul answers the implicit question of chapter 2 by exploring the practical meaning of the resurrection. In doing so he shows that the religion attacked in 2:8–23 is a parody of the truth. It struggles to attain heavenly worship, which is in fact given freely to all Christ's people. It focuses on the world and the body as the spheres where holiness operates, and ends up being both worldly and fleshly. The old taboos put the wild animals of lust and hatred (see 3:5, 8) into cages: there they remain, alive and dangerous, a constant threat to their captor. Paul's solution is more drastic: the animals are to be killed (3:5). The old method of holiness attacked symptoms: the true method goes for the root.

This subsection of the letter, then, places the Christian firmly in the New Age, and requires that he or she live appropriately.

[1] The problem with this – that there is no word for 'restrain' (NIV) or 'check' (RSV) – is eased if we understand *pros* as 'in relation to': they are of no value *in relation to, i.e.* in the effort to control, fleshly gratification.

In 3:1–4 Paul establishes the basis: Christians are already risen with Christ. In 3:5–11 he describes the life of the old age, and urges the Colossians to make a clean break with it. In 3:12–17 he encourages them to embrace the life of the new age; in 3:18 – 4:1 he applies this in detail to daily life in the family and place of work. Finally in 4:2–6 he exhorts them to constant prayer and Christian witness in the world.

The outstanding feature of this part of the letter is the sharp contrast between the old life and the new, as described in 3:5–11 and 3:12–17. It is salutary to ponder the characteristics of the one for a while, to sense its whole mood and style of life, and then to switch suddenly to the other. They are indeed worlds apart. In the one we find attitudes and behaviour that cause inevitable fragmentation in human society and even within individuals: in the other, a way of life which integrates both individual persons and groups of people. The former, in other words, steadily obliterates genuinely human existence: the latter enhances it.

Paul's appeal to abandon the first lifestyle and embrace the second has exactly appropriate theological foundations. He reminds the Colossians of who they now are because of God's grace. They are 'God's chosen people, holy and dearly loved', who have experienced his forgiveness at first hand (vv.12–13): they belong to the new humanity, which is being 'renewed in knowledge in the image of its Creator'. The chief characteristics of the old life are precisely those which grow up where these truths are not known or appreciated. Lust and anger feed on insecurity, attempting to overcome it by dominating other human beings, but always sinking more into fear and pride – which in turn cause further anxiety. The gospel goes to the root of this problem. The freeness of God's love attacks pride: its faithfulness, fear. The genuinely human existence which Paul commends cannot be reached except through belief in the forgiving love of God.

Nor can it be reached in isolation. 'Christian conduct is the result, not simply of the effort to be good, but of incorporation into the Body of Christ.'[1] Individualism, rightly prized by many Christians as a guard against the dangerous idea that mem-

---

[1] Moule, p.114: the whole sentence is in italics.

bership in the church makes individual belief and conduct a matter of secondary importance, can easily be twisted into the equally dangerous notion that membership in the church itself is of comparative insignificance. God intends Christian behaviour to be reinforced and upheld by the friendship, company, teaching, counselling and loving criticism of other Christians. Not to appreciate this is to lapse into that arrogant independence of one's fellow human beings – worse, one's fellow Christians – which is a sign not of the new life but of the old.

It has often been remarked that some of the details of this passage overlap not only with the parallels in Ephesians but with sections of other New Testament writings. With Colossians 3:5, 8, for instance, we may compare Mark 7:21–22; Romans 1:29–32; 1 Corinthians 5:10–11; 6:9–10; Galatians 5:19–21; Ephesians 5:3–6; 1 Thessalonians 4:3–8; 2 Timothy 3:2–5; James 1:21; 1 Peter 2:1; 4:3; with Colossians 3:12ff., Romans 5:2–5; Galatians 5:22–23; Titus 3:1–2; James 3:17; 2 Peter 1:5–7; and, with Colossians 3:18 – 4:1, Ephesians 5:21 – 6:9; Titus 2:2–10 and 1 Peter 2:18 – 3:7. It is much easier to suppose that all these passages reflect standard early Christian teaching, such as all new converts would receive, than to imagine that one of them is the source for all the others. These lists of 'vices' and 'virtues' have some features in common with non-Christian ethical catalogues of the period,[1] but are sharply distinguished from them by their specifically Christian motivations. The Jew attempted to keep the Torah to demonstrate his membership in the family of Abraham. The Stoic attempted to rise above passion to the state of total tranquillity. Paul urges his readers to copy God himself in glad, outgoing love, and so to discover in Christ what it means to be truly human.

i. Live in Christ, the risen Lord (3:1–4)

1–2. Paul has just drawn out the implications of dying with Christ (2:20–23); the Colossians have left behind the old age. Now he draws out the implications of having also risen with

---

[1] See the full discussion (e.g. of other lists of five vices and virtues, as here) in Schweizer, pp.182–191.

Christ. They have entered the new age, and, belonging there by right, do not have to struggle to attain the status of membership in God's people: they already have it. They must now simply allow its life to be worked out in them: *Since, then, you have been raised with Christ, set your hearts on* (literally, simply 'seek'[1]) *things above . . . Set your minds on things above, not on earthly things.*

The three focal points of this appeal are (a) the fact that Christ's people are already risen with him; (b) the appeal to an activity of the mind and will; (c) the object of that activity. The first point is to be amplified in verses 3 and 4, and we shall consider it presently. The second point makes a (no doubt deliberate) contrast with the spurious methods of holiness attacked in 2:8–23. Submission to the 'powers' and their outward regulations is essentially dehumanizing; mind and heart need not be in gear with what the body is required to do. God's purpose in Christ, as we saw in chapter 1, is to produce truly human beings, who find in the service of God a new integration of thought and action. The primacy, in Christian behaviour, of the attitude of the *mind* is of course no excuse for barren intellectualism; many Christians, however, make that danger an excuse for not giving the mind the place God intended it to have. Someone who truly understands who he or she is in Christ is further along the road to genuine holiness than someone who, in confusion, anxiously imagines that the new life is the result, rather than the starting-point, of the daily battle with temptation. We may compare 1:9–11, on which see the commentary.

The third point, the object of the 'seeking', the place where thoughts are to rest, is 'the things that are above', contrasted in verse 2 with 'the things that are on the earth'. Here again there is an implicit contrast with the religion of 2:16–23. But what are these 'heavenly things'? They are well set out in Philippians 4:8, and also in 3:12ff. of our present letter: the qualities of self-giving love *are* the chief characteristics of the life of heaven, because heaven is *where Christ is, seated at the right hand of God* (NIV is certainly wrong to omit the comma and so to make 'is seated' into a single expression). This phrase, particularly in its

---

[1] As in, *e.g.*, the instructive parallel Mt. 6:33.

allusion to Psalm 110, focuses attention on the sovereign rule which Christ now exercises. The command to aspire to the things of heaven is a command to meditate and dwell upon Christ's sort of life, and on the fact that he is now enthroned as the Lord of the world. The Bible does not say very much about heaven. But its central feature is clear: it is the place where the crucified Christ already reigns, where his people already have full rights of citizenship (Phil. 3:19ff.). To concentrate the mind on the character of Jesus Christ, on that unique blend of love and strength revealed in the Gospels, is to begin on earth to reflect the very life of heaven.

3–4. The commands to set mind and heart on 'the things above' are more powerfully reinforced in the next two verses. *For you died* (as in 2:11–12, 20), *and your life is now hidden with Christ in God.* This statement leaves several questions unanswered, so Paul continues: *When Christ, who is your[1] life, appears, then you also will appear with him in glory.* Here we have a full, if brief, description of the Christian's true status. With Christ, he has died, he is risen, and he will appear in glory. There is a perfect balance here between the 'already' and the 'not yet' that are so characteristic of Paul's teaching on the Christian life.[2] The new age has dawned, and Christians already belong to it. The old age, however, is not yet wound up, and until they die (or until the Lord 'appears' again in his second coming) their new life will be a secret truth, 'hidden' from view (from others, much of the time: often enough, from themselves too).

The life of Christians thus becomes part of the 'mystery', the secret plan of God, to be revealed to the world at the end of time: that life is not just 'hidden with Christ in God' (v.3), it actually *is* Christ himself (v.4), their hope of glory (1:27). As in Romans 8:18ff., or 1 John 3:1ff., the Christian hopes not merely

---

[1]Many MSS read 'our' (SO RSV, NEB). This might be preferred on the grounds that a scribe would be more likely to change it to 'your' to fit in with 'you' in the next part of the verse. But 'your' here is well supported by a wide range of MSS, and might have been altered to 'our' to avoid seeming to have Paul saying that Christ was their life, but by implication not his as well.

[2]For a good critique of those who have found here an un-Pauline emphasis on the 'already', see Lincoln, *Paradise* (above, p.108, n.3), pp.122–134.

for the coming of the Lord, but for the full revelation of what he or she already is. Then will it be seen with what faithful diligence and perseverance many outwardly 'unsuccessful' and forgotten Christian workers have served their Lord. Paul, the prisoner, an eccentric Jew to the Romans and a worse-than-Gentile traitor to the Jews, will be seen as Paul the apostle, the servant of the King. The Colossians, insignificant ex-pagans from a third-rate country town, will be seen in a glory which, if it were now to appear, one might be tempted to worship. This is how they are to regard their life, and on this foundation they are to build genuine holiness and Christian maturity.

ii. Knowledge and life renewed according to God's image (3:5–11)

The first section of the ethical appeal is primarily negative, its focal points being the commands 'put to death . . .' and 'rid yourselves . . .' (vv.5, 8). These verbs introduce two lists of vices, one relating to sexual sin, the other to sins of anger. The two lists are classic statements of the ways in which Christians can be untrue to themselves and, more importantly, to God. By bluntly naming sins which are all too often excused or glossed over with euphemisms, Paul sets a clear standard for the church both ancient and modern. Many Christians tend to concentrate on one list or the other: one knows of Christian communities that would be appalled at the slightest sexual irregularity but which are nests of malicious intrigue, backbiting, gossip and bad temper, and, conversely, of others where people are so concerned to live in untroubled harmony with each other that they tolerate flagrant immorality. The gospel, however, leaves no room for behaviour of either sort.

5. If Christians have already died and risen again with Christ, *whatever belongs to your earthly nature* must be *put to death*. The word *therefore* shows, as so often in Paul, that the command is dependent on the previous statements. The new life, to be revealed fully on the last day (v.4), is to let itself be seen in advance, in the present time, in Christian behaviour.[1] 'Your

---

[1] So Williams, p.125.

earthly nature' is a potentially misleading phrase. Paul is not advocating a sort of Buddhist abstraction from ordinary human life, but rather the abandoning of a way of life that is 'earthly' as opposed to 'heavenly' in the sense indicated by verses 1–4, *i.e.* that belongs to the old age and not to the new. Literally the phrase could be translated 'the members (or 'limbs') which are upon the earth'; Paul probably intends this as a vivid metaphor, as in Matthew 5:29–30; 18:8–9. Practices such as these are like a gangrenous limb to the eyes of a surgeon: they must be cut off before they infect the whole person.

The list moves from the specific to the general. The word here translated *sexual immorality* refers to any intercourse outside marriage: in the ancient world, as in the modern, intercourse with a prostitute would be a specific, and in pagan culture a frequent, instance of this. *Impurity* highlights the contamination of character effected by immoral behaviour. The word rendered *lust* could refer to any overmastering passion, but regularly, as here, indicates uncontrolled sexual urges. *Evil desires* (the word 'evil' is added because 'desire' by itself, which is what the Greek word means, could be used in a neutral sense) is the state which logically precedes lust. It is perhaps important to note, as is clearly implied by Hebrews 4:15, that experiencing sexual temptation is not itself sinful. Sin begins when the idea of illicit gratification, presented to the mind in temptation, is not at once put to death, but is instead fondled and cherished.[1] Behind this stage, in turn, there is *greed*: another general term, here it refers to unchecked hunger for physical pleasure, which is the breeding-ground for more specific evil desires. Paul boldly unmasks this covetousness: it *is idolatry*. Literal idol-worship, of course, formed the setting for a good deal of the sort of behaviour here criticized, but that is only an illustration of the basic point. All such greed places at the centre of one's attention and devotion that which is not God. In turning from the source of life, those who follow other paths are actually pursuing death (*cf.* Rom. 1:21ff., 32; 6:21), as the next verse indicates.

---

[1] The AV's 'inordinate affection' is now a misleading translation, because 'affection' has come to refer to friendship and love, and their outward expressions, rather than (as in the seventeenth century) to inner desires. NEB's 'foul cravings' is perhaps too strong, and hence too restricted in scope.

If these vices are not, eventually, to kill the one who practises them, they must themselves be 'put to death'. The old word 'mortify', used here in AV, has now acquired exactly the wrong sense, implying just such a regime of ascetic discipline as Paul has declared to be worse than useless (2:20–23). 'Mortification' like that avoids dealing directly with the sin itself. Paul's recommended treatment is simpler and more drastic. To put something to death you must cut off its lines of supply: it is futile and self-deceiving to bemoan one's inability to resist the last stage of a temptation when earlier stages have gone by unnoticed, or even eagerly welcomed. This does not mean setting up a new hedge around the law, such as branding all theatrical performances (or whatever) as inherently 'sinful'. Rather, every Christian has the responsibility, before God, to investigate the lifelines of whatever sins are defeating him personally, and to cut them off without pity. Better that than have them eventually destroy him.

6. Destruction, indeed, will be the result for those who disregard the warning: *because of these, the wrath of God is coming.*[1] It is not the case that God happens to dislike this sort of behaviour and so has decided, as it were arbitrarily, to punish it. On the contrary. 'The wrath of God', it hardly needs saying, is not a malicious or capricious anger,[2] but the necessary reaction of true holiness, justice and goodness to wickedness, exploitation and evil of every kind. This wrath begins to take effect in the squalid and degrading effects of sin itself (Rom. 1:18–32). But that process is not the whole of 'wrath': it leads to the final judgment (see Rom. 1:32; 2:1–16). The present tense in Colossians 3:6 refers, perhaps deliberately, to both these senses of God's wrath, though 'is coming' (NIV, RSV) emphasizes the future aspect. Part of the horror of hell, it appears, is that those who consciously and continually choose sin instead of God become

[1] The majority of MSS add, as in Eph. 5:6, 'upon the sons of disobedience'. To retain this phrase allows 'in them' and 'in these ones' (*en hois* and *en toutois*) in v.7 to refer to different antecedents, which seems preferable to omitting it and making them both refer to 'because of which' (*di' ha*) in v.6. (See Metzger, pp.624 f., against, *e.g.*, O'Brien, p.173.) Vv.6–7 will then mean 'because of these things God's wrath is coming upon the sons of disobedience, *among whom* (*en hois*) you also once walked, when you lived *in these things* (*en toutois*)'.

[2] As could be implied by JB: 'all this is the sort of behaviour that makes God angry'.

less and less human, until all that ennobles them as creatures made in God's image has, by their own choice, been altogether obliterated, beyond hope or pity.

It is perhaps along these lines that the difficult doctrine of hell may be comprehensibly stated today, in opposition to the current notion that hell does not exist, or that if it does it will at the last be untenanted, or that even if some will remain there it is in bad taste to mention the fact. Unless we are to rob human beings of all meaningful responsibility for their actions, and to underplay the utter holiness of God, hell must always be at least a possibility. The presence in the world of much dehumanizing evil – dehumanizing to its practitioners even more than to its sufferers – indicates clearly enough how we may understand it. Those who make evil a way of life begin to lose their humanity, begin (in other words) to die, even while they are alive: witness the dead eyes of the miser, the torturer, the prostitute. Paul's constant emphasis on full, genuine Christian humanity casts a clear shadow over non-Christian existence. Those who choose to live without God will one day find that they have forfeited their likeness to him.

7. Paul knew only too well that the great majority of ex-pagan converts would find in verse 5 a description of their own former way of life (compare 1 Cor. 6:10–11). *You used to walk in these ways,* he says ('walk' referring, as usual, to conduct in general; see above on 1:10), *in the life you once lived.* 'To live' is more fundamental, for Paul, than 'to walk' (compare Gal. 5:25): the 'walk', the actual conduct, reveals the 'life', the settled state of existence. And in the Greek the last words of the verse (*en toutois*) are perhaps contemptous: 'when your life consisted of such wretched things as these'.[1]

8. *But now* (a classic Pauline way of indicating the transition from the old life to the new: *cf.* 1:22) *you must rid yourselves of all such things as these.* 'These' may refer to the list of verse 5 as well as that of verse 8. They must be 'put behind you' (J. B. Phillips).

---

[1]Many MSS have *autois* (simply 'them') for *toutois* ('these'), but the latter should be preferred as the harder reading. For the meaning in connection with the different readings in v.6, see p.135, n.1, above.

When a tide of passion or a surge of anger is felt, it must be dealt with as the alien intruder it really is, and turned out of the house as having no right to be there at all, let alone to be giving orders. This is often harder than it sounds, but it must be constantly attempted, in reliance on the grace which continually renews the life of the Christian (v. 10; *cf.* 2 Cor. 4:16).

It is far easier to drift into a sin which one does not know by name than consciously to choose one whose very title should be repugnant to a Christian. The list in verse 8 is another ugly one: *anger*, the continuous state of smouldering or seething hatred; *rage*, when this state breaks out in actual angry deeds or words; *malice*, a word which in the Greek can simply mean 'evil', but which here probably has the overtone of 'evil intended to cause hurt'; *slander*, speech which puts malice into practical effect (the Greek is *blasphēmia*, speech which dishonours God himself – in this instance, by reviling a human being made in his image); *and filthy language*, words which, either by their foul association or their abusive intent, contaminate both speaker and hearers. All such things are to be put away *from your lips*: one cannot always prevent angry or hateful thoughts from springing into one's head, but they should be dealt with firmly before they turn into words. It is not 'healthy', as is sometimes supposed, to allow such thoughts to find expression. It is certainly healthy to recognize and face up to one's own anger or frustration, and to search for proper and creative ways of dealing with it. But words do not merely convey information or let off steam. They change situations and relationships, often irrevocably. They can wound as well as heal. Like wild plants blown by the wind, hateful words can scatter their seeds far and wide, giving birth to more anger wherever they land.

9–10. Among the most dangerous seeds are untruths: *Do not lie to each other.* Truth is often inconvenient, untidy or embarrassing, and we are constantly tempted to bend it into a less awkward shape. But this too is out of place for the Christian, *since you have taken off your old self with its practices and have put on the new self.* This does not merely mean that Christ demands a new standard of life from his redeemed people. The new self *is being renewed . . . in the image of its Creator.* The behaviour outlined in verses 5 and 8 is characteristic of distorted humanity. Being itself out of shape, it tends to twist everything else – people, by manipulation or anger; facts, by lying – to make them fit in with its own distortions. The humanity which has been straightened out according to the perfect model, that of Christ (1:15–20; 2:6) has no excuse for such behaviour. The standard now is the life of heaven (3:1–4). They do not behave like that there.

But is this ethical appeal realistic? Paul answers with a strong affirmative, undergirding ethics with theology. Though it may not always feel like it, those who have joined the family of Christ have become different people. They have 'taken off' the old solidarity, the old humanity, like a shabby set of clothes. 'Self' in NIV is misleadingly individualistic, since the idea, here as in Romans 6:6, is much more than merely individual; it could also imply the false idea that 'self' and 'Christ' will always be opposed, whereas in truth it is one's true self, one's full humanity, that emerges once the shackles of the old humanity are thrown off. This metaphor of 'taking off' clothes does not mean simply the making of good resolutions or promises to behave differently. It is the action – itself the reflex, in human experience, of God's action in grace by the Spirit – of leaving one family, or household, and moving lock, stock and barrel into another, where a different rule of life obtains.

Paul here may well be alluding to the familiar picture of the candidate for baptism, who, symbolizing this transfer of solid-arities, exchanges his old clothes for new ones. ('Taking off the old humanity' and 'putting on the new humanity' are aorist participles in the Greek, indicating actions that are unique and unrepeatable.) The old humanity is the solidarity of Adam's people: compare Romans 5:12–21 and (growing out of that paragraph) 6:1 – 7:6. The new humanity is the solidarity of those who are incorporated into, and hence patterned on, the Messiah who is himself the true Man (the same passages in Romans could be cited again). This new humanity is therefore (if we translate the passage literally) 'renewed according to the image of the one who created it'. At last, in Christ, human beings can be what God intended them to be. This passage clearly looks back to 1:15–20; the intention of creation is fulfilled in redemption, and, conversely, redemption is understood as new creation. As in Paul's reported prayer of 1:9ff., this renewal is put into effect not only in outward actions but also, and as a prior necessity, *in knowledge*: the phrase literally means *'into knowledge'*, implying that the 'renewal' spoken of is to *result in the true knowledge of God* – and, perhaps, of good and evil also. Practical Christianity is founded on the full recognition of truth about God and about oneself. And, since this is the foundation, truth is also demonstrated in the full structure; since the ethic Paul is commending produces individual and corporate stability and integration, it is in a measure self-authenticating.

11. In this new community and solidarity which the Colossians have now joined (*'here'*: the word indicates a place, presumably the family of Christ's people, with the emphasis being 'one doesn't behave like that *here'*) *there is no Greek or Jew, circumcised or uncircumcised, barbarian, Scythian, slave or free.* These intermingled distinctions of race, ancestral religion, class and caste provide the best soil for that mutual suspicion and distrust which turn into the vices listed in verse 8. These divisions were of great importance in the ancient world. The spread of Greek civilization after the conquests of Alexander the Great meant that the 'Greek', whether from Greece itself, Egypt, Asia Minor or anywhere else, could regard himself as a member of a privileged group, somewhat like those who speak a major European language in much of the modern world. He would look down on the circumscribed nationalism of the Jew who insisted on preserving and clinging to his old culture, just as the Jew, fiercely conscious of God's election of Israel and of the shallowness and moral darkness of Greek polytheism, would despise him. These differences were accentuated by the physical mark of the male Jew: circumcision was prized in Israel and mocked by her enemies. 'Barbarians' is a contemptuous word used by Greeks for anyone who did not speak their language: the Scythians (from the then little-known northern reaches of Asia) were the extreme examples of barbarians, little better than savages. The distinction between slave and free, of course, ran through ancient society just as obviously as a colour bar still does in some areas today (whether or not officially sanctioned), and with just as damaging an effect on human relations and self-esteem. The ancient world, just like the modern, was an elaborate network of prejudice, suspicion and arrogance, so ingrained as to be thought natural and normal.

These distinctions, Paul declares with a breath-taking challenge, have become irrelevant in Christ. The 'powers of the world' did indeed hold the human race in their grip, as men and women allowed their habits of thought and action to be dominated by them. Paul's counter-claim, set before the church as a still unfinished agenda, is that these barriers and habits are, in terms of God's proper will for his human creatures, neither natural nor normal. They are, ultimately, a denial of the creation of humankind in the image of God. That is not to say that differences cease to exist (any more than the male-female distinction ceases to exist, in the similar list of Gal. 3:28). It is to say that differences of background, nationality, colour, language, social standing and so forth must be regarded as irrelevant to the question of the love, honour and respect that are to be shown to individuals and groups.

Instead, *Christ is all, and in all*. In another echo of 1:15-20 Paul grounds his challenge in this double statement of the universal significance of Christ. On the one hand, he is 'all things' (or 'the totality'[1]): in other words, he, the pre-existent image of God, is the one whose being underlies all human nature of whatever category (Jew or Greek, civilized or uncivilized, high or low born). Only a Christology as fully insistent as Paul's on both the divinity and the humanity of Jesus Christ can undergird this claim, that in him there can be no barriers between human beings. On the other hand, he is 'in all' – probably, 'in all people' (taking *en pasin* as masculine: a second neuter might seem redundant, and the context refers more specifically to people). Wherever one looks, one sees Christ. When an elderly person is ignored, Christ is ignored; where a lively teenager is snubbed, he is snubbed; where a poor or coloured person (or, for that matter, a rich or white one) is treated with contempt, the reproach falls on him. There must therefore be mutual welcome

---

[1] Retaining the Greek article *ta*, partly on good MS evidence and partly because, while it makes good sense, it would be easy for a scribe to omit.

and respect within the people of God. Nobody must allow prejudices from their pre-Christian days to distort the new humanity which God has created in and through the New Man.

The letter to Philemon again provides a good example of this theology put into effect.

iii. Do all in the name of the Lord Jesus (3:12–17)

12. The mood changes from negative to positive: it is like coming out of fog into sunlight. The same motivation that prompts the Christian to abandon the old ways of life encourages her or him to embrace the new ways: hence Paul begins with a typical *Therefore* . . . As God's new humanity (3:10) the church is God's true Israel, to whom have been transferred the epithets which formerly belonged to Israel according to the flesh. Christians are *God's chosen people, holy and dearly loved.* God has assured them in Christ that their membership in his people, their being 'set apart' for his service (that is the underlying meaning of 'holy'), depends not on their goodness but on his grace, not on their lovableness but on his love. These titles are not only used of Israel in the Old Testament, but also of Jesus Christ in the New: he is the 'chosen' one (1 Pet. 2:4, 6), the holy one (Jn. 6:69; Acts 4:27, 30, *etc.*), the one supremely beloved by the Father (Mt. 3:17; Eph. 1:6, *etc.*). It is in him that Christians find their identity as God's people. Verses 12–17 contain echoes of the earlier Christological sections of the letter, applying here to those who belong to Christ what is there said of him personally.

Having taken off the shabby 'clothes' appropriate for the old age, the Colossians are to be fitted out with beautiful new robes, appropriate for their new position. They are not accustomed to such finery, but God's loving and gracious choice of them makes it fitting that they should now wear it. Paul earlier (1:11) prayed that this sort of character would appear in the Colossians; he now urges them (*clothe yourselves* . . .) to make his prayer come true. They are to 'put on' a deep sensitivity to the needs and sorrows of others (*compassion* in NIV and RSV compresses into one word two words which together refer to an understanding sympathy with others that affects one's innermost being). This heartfelt compassion is to be coupled with *kindness* – 'the art of being a dear', as Lord Hailsham once paraphrased the Latin *caritas*; it is strange, in view of the emphasis given by Paul to this basic virtue, how often it is regarded in practice as inessential. And if 'kindness' is a Christlike attitude towards others, *humility* is the Christlike attitude towards oneself, supremely exemplified in that readiness to forgo his own rights which led the Son of God to the incarnation and cross (Phil. 2:5-11). The last two qualities (bringing the total to five, balancing the lists of five vices in vv.5, 8) are the positive and negative outworkings of kindness and humility: *gentleness* is the effect of meek humility on one's *approach* to other people, whereas *patience* is the effect of that humble kindness on one's *reaction* to other people. The first forswears rudeness or arrogance; the second, resentment and anger.

13. These virtues are at once given practical application: *bear with each other* – *i.e.* restrain your natural reaction towards odd or difficult people, let them be themselves – *and forgive whatever grievances you may have against one another*, whether old feuds from pre-Christian days which might jeopardize the new-found fellowship, or problems and squabbles which might arise (Paul was a realist) within the new community itself. The underlying principle is clear: *forgive as the Lord forgave you*. Paul here makes two points, echoing (perhaps intentionally) the parable of the Unforgiving Servant in Matthew 18:23-35. First, it is utterly inappropriate for one who knows the joy and release of being forgiven to refuse to share that blessing with another. Second, it is highly presumptuous to refuse to forgive one whom Christ himself has already forgiven.

14. The final garment to be put on is love itself, which will hold the rest in place: *and over all these virtues put on love, which binds them all together in perfect unity*. That, at least, is one possible meaning of the Greek, though in fact the sentence is more ambiguous than NIV allows. The final clause, literally translated, is simply 'the bond of perfection', with the word 'bond' possibly carrying the metaphorical meaning of an outer garment holding the others together, or simply a brooch or clasp which does the same job. The sentence could equally well mean that love is the characteristic (there is no word in the Greek corresponding to 'virtue' in NIV) which binds the whole *church* (as opposed to the other virtues) together. The frequent parallels in secular literature to the idea of a supreme virtue acting as the unifying principle for the others mean that NIV's interpretation is probably to be preferred, indicting a specifically Christian viewpoint over against other systems of ethics. 'Love' never has this supreme position in other systems, not even (for instance) in the admirable list of virtues found in the Qumran *Community Rule*.[1] The other virtues, pursued without love, become distorted and unbalanced.

15. When love has its full effect in the community it will result in peace: *Let the peace of Christ rule in your hearts, since as members of one body you were called to peace.* The second clause (which RSV renders, more literally, 'to which indeed you were called in the one body') indicates that 'peace' here is not the inward, individual peace of mind which accompanies humble, confident trust in God's love, but a peace which characterizes the community, the 'body', as a whole. 'One body' here is a simple metaphor, the church being understood as a single living organism whose 'members' (the word is supplied by NIV to fill out the sense) must act in harmony; but it is hard to imagine that Paul is not alluding to the idea of the church as *Christ's* body, as (*e.g.*) in 1:18; 2:19.

The peace which is to characterize the church is not to be a mere outward absence of hostility. It is to be 'the peace of Christ', which must become the deciding factor (the Greek word for 'rule' probably has the overtone of someone acting as umpire or arbitrator) 'in your hearts': whatever disagreements or mutual suspicions occur in the church, they are to be dealt with at the deepest level, by all parties allowing the fact of their unity in Christ to settle the issue in their hearts. The *pax Christiana* is to prevail in the church, as the *pax Romana* did in the world of Paul's day, allowing its inhabitants to pursue their respective callings without the constant threat of war. This vision of the

[1] 1QS 4:3–6 (Vermes, p.76).

143

church's life prompts Paul to add once more *and be thankful* (see above, on 1:3, 12, *etc.*). Love, peace and gratitude reinforce each other, and set the context within which the exhortations of the next verses may be obeyed.

16. The tasks Paul described as his own in 1:28 are not his alone: they are for the whole church, *as you teach and admonish one another*, in the mutual forgiveness and trust of verses 12–15. This activity is further described in two ways. First, it is to be achieved by letting *the word of Christ dwell in you richly*. The first phrase could refer to the teaching about Jesus Christ, stories such as we now have in the Gospels; and certainly there is something attractively wholesome in Williams' comment, 'be at home in the Gospel story, and let it be at home in you, so that it may be always ready for use'.[1] But it more likely refers to the gospel message announcing what God has done in and through Christ, which was set out in 1:15–20 and applied to the Colossian situation in 2:6ff.; or, just possibly, to the word which Christ speaks in the present by his Spirit. None of these possibilities, of course, should be played off against another: the gospel message and the word given in the present are both recognized as authentic by their conformity with the man Jesus himself. This word is to dwell in them 'richly': the church is to be stocked with good teaching as a palace is filled with treasures. The teaching is to be *with all wisdom*: the 'word' concerns Christ, Wisdom himself (2:3, *etc.*), and will be characterized by wisdom in the teachers.

This ministry of teaching and admonishing is to be part of a life of thankfulness that overflows into song: *as you sing psalms, hymns and spiritual songs with gratitude in your hearts to God.* Linking the two parts of the verse in this way suggests that the singing is not the sole or primary means of teaching, though Christian hymns and songs have often been a powerful means of implanting and clarifying Christian truth. Rather, the ministry of instruction should always be seen as one part of a total life characterized by grateful worship. 'To God' could go with 'singing' instead of 'gratitude'. But NIV and RSV probably express

[1]Williams, p. 142.

Paul's meaning. 'In your hearts' gives the location, not of the singing (though it should of course be heartfelt), but of the gratitude.

The three different categories of song in this verse are not easy to distinguish. Older writers suggested that 'psalms' were probably accompanied, and that 'songs', being a more general word than 'hymns', is qualified with the adjective 'spiritual' to distinguish it from secular singing. 'Psalms' may actually refer to the Christian use of the Old Testament psalter, but should not be restricted to that; the early church was prolific in its adaptation of Old Testament themes to Christian use (see, *e.g.*, Rev. 5:9–10; 15:3–4, *etc.*), and in its composition of new material (see, perhaps, Phil. 2:6–11; Col. 1:15–20; 1 Tim. 3:16). Together these three terms indicate a variety and richness of Christian singing which should neither be stereotyped into one mould nor restricted simply to weekly public worship.

17. Paul now closes the circle which began at 2:6. *And whatever you do, whether in word or deed, do it all in the name of the Lord Jesus.* Acting 'in someone's name' means both representing him and being empowered to do so. Paul's exhortation is therefore a salutary check on behaviour ('can I really do this, if I am representing the Lord Jesus?') and an encouragement to persevere with difficult tasks undertaken for him, knowing that necessary strength will be provided. And again Paul adds the characteristic emphasis: *giving thanks to God the Father through him.* The centre of Christian living is grateful worship, which is to affect 'whatever we do': since 'all things' have been created through Christ and also, in principle, redeemed through him, Christians can do all that they do, whether it be manual work, political activity, raising a family, writing a book, playing tennis, or whatever, in his name and with gratitude. Jesus, the true divine and human image of God, the one whose cross secured our reconciliation, is the reason for our gratitude, and the one 'through whom' we can now offer that gratitude to the Father himself.

iv. New life – at home (3:18 – 4:1)

Putting the life of the new age into practice begins at home. If a sense of anti-climax is felt on moving from the sublime picture of the worshipping church in 3:15–17 to the almost mundane instructions of 3:18 – 4:1, that is perhaps a sign that we have not fully integrated belief and practice. It is clear from the numerous parallels to this section in other early Christian literature[1] that the early church took seriously the necessity of living Christianly in the place where, for better or for worse, one is truly oneself. And these terse sentences focus on just that: how to be truly oneself, in the Lord, as a member of the new humanity – and how to set the other members of one's family free to be truly themselves. 'If the home is to be a means of grace it must be a place of *rules* . . . the alternative to rule is not freedom but the unconstitutional (and often unconscious) tyranny of the most selfish member.'[2] As in improvised music, spontaneity and freedom do not mean playing out of tune.

But should Paul's tunes, so to speak, be our tunes? We meet here, not for the first time, the question of the applicability of what he says to twentieth-century life. This question sometimes surfaces in another guise, namely, how specifically Christian are these instructions?

It is true that pagans and Jews at this period compiled household rules which are in some respects parallel to what we find here.[3] But this does not mean that Paul is simply telling his converts to conform to prevailing contemporary standards. Christian ethics and secular standards are, of course, not altogether different: since all people are created in God's image, with an innate sense of God's standards (see Rom. 1:32; 2:1–16), the rule of life which will restore that image to its proper glory (3:10) need not scrap all non-Christian values and begin over again, but will be able to build on, and bring to full maturity, what is best in the world outside the church. In addition, it is clear from (*e.g.*) Romans 12:9 and 13:1–7 that Paul expected Christians to recognize the ordinary standards of 'good' and

---

[1]See Eph. 5:21 – 6:9; Tit. 2:2–10; 1 Pet. 2:18 – 3:7; 1 Clem. 21: 6–8; Ign. *Pol.* 4:1 – 6:2; Polycarp *To the Philippians* 4:2 – 6:1.

[2]C. S. Lewis 'The Sermon and the Lunch', in *Undeceptions: Essays on Theology and Ethics*, ed. W. Hooper (Bles, 1971), p.237. The whole short piece is a gem of realistic teaching on home life.

[3]Full details, and bibliography, may be found in Lohse, Schweizer or O'Brien, *ad loc.*

'bad', to avoid giving needless offence to non-Christian society. But the differences between Paul and his pagan contemporaries are as clear as the parallels. Paul has thoroughly Christianized the code, not just by adding 'in the Lord' at certain points, but by balancing carefully the duties and responsibilities of the various family members so that the stronger parties have duties as well as rights, and those who are in a position of submission are treated as responsible human beings, with rights as well as duties. He thus sharpens up, in one area of practical life, the standards set out in 3:5–14.

It is, in fact, extremely unlikely that Paul, having warned the young Christians against conforming their lives to the present world, would now require just that of them after all. Nor does he. The Stoics (who provide some of the closest pagan parallels to these household lists) based their teaching on the law of nature: this is the way the world is, so this is how you must live in harmony with it. Paul bases his on the law of the *new* nature: Christ releases you to be truly human, and you must now learn to express your true self according to the divine pattern, not in self-assertion but in self-giving.

The problem, of course, is that Paul is often suspected of saying something else: of entrenching, in particular, the dominance of husbands over wives. It is perhaps verse 18 which has caused many writers to argue that what Paul writes here is relative, not absolute, and that the proper application of the passage is that we in our turn must think out quite different ways of expressing Christian love in the modern world. But it would be a bold person who would argue, in the face of modern society, that the contemporary non-Christian world offers a better model for marriage and family life than that provided by the ancient world, still less than that suggested by Paul. The solution is to be found, rather, in seeing just what it is that Paul does, and does not, say.

18–19. He offers a careful balance. Neither party is to be arrogant or domineering: *Wives, submit to your husbands, as is fitting in the Lord. Husbands, love your wives and do not be harsh with them.* The 'submission' here is not that of the slave, or the doormat. The equality of women and men before the Lord, of which Paul wrote in Galatians 3:28, has not been retracted: but neither does it mean identity of role or function. The wife must forgo the temptation to rule her husband's life, using perhaps one of the many varieties of domestic blackmail; the husband must ensure that his love for his wife, like Christ's for his people, always puts her interests first (see the fuller statement in Eph. 5:21–33). In particular, he must scrupulously avoid the temptation to resent her being the person she is, to become bitter or angry when she turns out to be, like him, a real human being, and not merely the projection of his own hopes or fantasies. It is when husbands and wives understand these guidelines and live by them that they are truly free: free to mature and develop, within the creative context of mutual love and respect.

20–21. In addressing children as members of the church in their own right, and in giving them both responsibilities and rights, Paul is again allowing the gospel to break new ground. *Children, obey your parents in everything, for this pleases the Lord. Fathers, do not embitter your children, or they will become discouraged.* In a couple of crisp sentences Paul has said, in essence, what thousands of books on the upbringing of children have struggled to express. Sometimes verse 20 has been over-emphasized, and verse 21 forgotten, in the zeal of parents not to spare the rod lest they spoil the child. Sometimes verse 21 has been over-stressed, and the rights of the individual child allowed to range free, trampling the rights of family, friends, neighbours and anyone else in the way, for fear lest young life be crushed or twisted. Both sides are clearly necessary. Children need discipline; so do parents. The word 'fathers' can refer to parents of both sexes, though it may well have an eye to the importance of the father's role, within God's created order, in the upbringing of children.

'Embitter' is literally 'arouse', usually in the bad sense of 'provoke'. Paul refers to the constant nagging or belittling of a child (a sure sign of insecurity (see 3:8), this time on the part of the parent), the refusal to allow children to be people in their own right instead of carbon copies of their parents or their parents' fantasies. Children treated like this became 'discouraged' or 'dispirited': hearing continually, both verbally and non-verbally, that they are of little value, they come to believe it, and either sink down in obedient self-hatred or over-react with boastful but anxious self-assertion. The parents' duty is, in effect, to live out the gospel to the child: that is, to assure their children that they are loved and accepted and valued for who they are, not for who they ought to be, should have been, or might (if only they would try a little harder) become. Obedience must never be made the condition of parental 'love'; a 'love' so conditioned would not deserve the name. When the parent is obedient to the vocation of genuine love, the child's obedience may become, like that of the Christian to God, a glad and loving response. Such obedience is 'pleasing to the Lord' (as the Greek expresses it), not merely because he desires order but because he wants all his people to follow the often paradoxical, self-denying, Christlike road to true and mature selfhood.

22. Paul has made it clear that the duties of members of families are 'in the Lord': and, in the extended section addressed to *slaves* (vv.22–25: it is sometimes suggested that this section has something to do with Onesimus' being sent with the letter, but it is hard to see why), he makes this point in no fewer than five different ways.

First, they are told to *obey your earthly masters in everything*: they are to be thoroughgoing in their obedience; *and do it, not only when their eye is on you and to win their favour, but with sincerity of heart and reverence for the Lord* (many MSS read 'God', perhaps to avoid confusion between the Lord (Jesus) and the 'lord', *i.e.* master, of the slave: the same word, *kyrios*, could indicate either). Here the point, equally applicable at all levels of human labour, is that the Christian at work must be a whole person, totally given to the task in hand, not merely doing the minimum required to avoid rebuke, with a show of effort when one is being observed. That attitude shows no reverence for the Lord who has called all his people to full, single-hearted human living. Even if they are treated like animals or worse, slaves are still to regard themselves as fully human beings.

23–24. Second, *whatever you do, work at it with all your heart, as working for the Lord, not for men.* The task may appear unimportant or trivial, but the person doing it is never that, and he or she has the opportunity to turn the job into an act of worship. This attitude cannot be motivated by earthly reward, and so cannot be distracted if such prospects seem remote: *since you know that you will receive an inheritance from the Lord as a reward.* One should properly read *'the* inheritance'; the reference is clearly to the life of the age to come. This is ironic, since in earthly terms slaves could not inherit property. Here, then, is the third point: the 'master' in heaven will reward you. The fourth one is perhaps not to be taken (with NIV) as a statement (*It is the Lord Christ that you are serving*) but, as is equally possible in the Greek, as a command: 'Serve the Lord Christ!' The force of this unusual phrase (Paul nowhere else allows the titles 'Lord' and 'Christ' to stand together without the name 'Jesus' as well) could be brought out by a paraphrase: 'so work for the true Master – Christ!'

25. The final reason for the slave's obedience functions, in the parallel in Ephesians 6:5–9, as a warning to masters. The point, however, is equally relevant in its context here. If one is serving Christ, one need not fear, as with earthly masters, that those who cover up shoddy work by putting on a good show in the boss's presence will get away with it, or that the master's own favourites will be rewarded however hard others may work. No: *anyone who does wrong will be repaid for his wrong, and there is no favouritism.* This last idea, repeated by Paul in other contexts (*e.g.* Rom. 2:11), is a commonplace of Jewish and Christian views of God's justice. The slave has thus both encouragement and warning: he need not imagine that being a Christian will excuse poor or half-hearted work.

4:1. The balance between the pairs of exhortations is again striking, in keeping with a letter emphasizing the dignity of all human beings. *Masters, provide your slaves with what is right and fair, because you know that you also have a Master in heaven.* Paul does not protest against the institution of slavery. That would be about as useful, for him, as a modern preacher fulminating against the internal combustion engine. His approach is subtler. He has found a fixed point on which to stand, from which to move the world: slaves too are human beings with rights. To talk of 'justice' and 'fairness' (properly the word means 'equality') in relation to slaves would sound extraordinary to most slave-owners of the ancient world. Masters, however, are themselves slaves of the one Master.

In whatever role, then, a Christian finds himself or herself, at home or at work, life can and must be lived 'for the Lord', and in harmony with one's fellow human beings. The rules which facilitate this state create true freedom.[1] The section therefore provides the necessary grounding for the wide-ranging instructions of 3:1–17.

v. New life – in the world (4:2–6)

This short section has two important functions within the letter as a whole. First, the life of the new humanity 'in the Lord' is not something merely to be enjoyed for its own sake. The Colossian church has new responsibilities as well as privileges. Secondly, and in consequence, Paul is drawing the letter towards its appropriate close; having begun with thanksgiving for God's world-wide work through the gospel (1:3–8), his thoughts turn again to that work and his part in it. But he does not thereby turn away from the Colossians. He claims them as partners, setting before them in general terms the tasks appropriate to them as a new community, in Christ and in Colosse (1:2). This section thus echoes 1:24 – 2:5, suggesting that Paul intended the latter as a bridge between his introduction of himself and the letter's main central section.

2. As one would expect from 1:3ff., these instructions focus on fundamentals: *Devote yourselves to prayer, being watchful and thankful.* It is possible that 'watchful' refers obliquely to the church's 'watching' for the Lord's return; more likely that, as in Matthew 26:41, it means 'stay awake', 'keep alert'. The connection here with thanksgiving (see on 1:3–8, 12b, *etc.*) may suggest the threefold rhythm: intercession, 'watching' for answers to

---

[1] A superb treatment of the subject of human freedom, very relevant to all the preceding section, may be found in S. C. Neill, *A Genuinely Human Existence*, ch.9 (pp.214–233).

prayer, and thanksgiving when answers appear. As children of the day (see 1 Thes. 5:4–11), Christians are to keep awake, looking out on the sleeping world which, as the object of God's love, is also to be the object of his people's 'devoted', *i.e.* regular, steady and thorough prayer.

3. These prayers will include specific intercessions, such as the reciprocation of Paul's prayer (1:9ff.) for them: *and pray for us, too, that God may open a door for our message.* The 'door' could be that which admits Gentiles to the people of God, or possibly the prison door that will open to let Paul and his message out into the world; it is more likely, however, that Paul refers to the 'door' that allows the word of God (the phrase literally means 'a door for the word') into the hearts, minds and lives of individuals and communities (*cf.* Acts 14:27; 1 Cor. 16:9; 2 Cor. 2:12). The 'word' is here personified, like the gospel (more fully, 'the word of the truth of the gospel') in 1:5–6. Here, as there, God is at work through the apostolic preaching, and this work of God must be supported and reinforced by the appropriate weapons, the intercessions of his people. The content of this 'word', in keeping with earlier references in the letter (1:26–27; 2:2), is further defined when Paul says *so that we may proclaim the mystery of Christ.* This phrase is to be understood in the light of earlier passages in the letter; it is the secret plan of God for the salvation of the whole world as this has now been made known in and through Jesus Christ. It is the mystery which consists in Christ – not merely in him as an individual, but in the wide implications of who he is and what he has achieved. A message, however, which challenges the power structures of the present age is always dangerous to proclaim: hence *for which I am in chains.* Paul's sufferings and present imprisonment were therefore, as he indicated in 1:24, part and parcel of his apostolic vocation, which itself was bound up with the mystery of Christ, and of the ushering in of the new age.

4. The NIV has not quite brought out the full force of the next sentence: *pray that I may proclaim it clearly, as I should.* The verb translated 'proclaim it clearly' literally means 'reveal' or 'make manifest', and belongs closely with 'mystery'. Paul must not

simply explain everything with clarity. He must announce, and so 'reveal', the mystery of Christ. He is under obligation to do so in such a way as to bring true knowledge and understanding to his hearers (see on 1:24 – 2:5).

5. The Colossians are to ensure that their lives and speech reflect that same mystery, the hidden wisdom of God. *Be wise in the way you act* is literally 'walk in wisdom', that is, follow Christ as God's pattern for full and authentic human living. Their lives are to reflect this wisdom *towards outsiders*.[1] Paul knew only too well (1 Cor. 10:32) the importance of giving the world no reason to criticize or gossip about the behaviour of Christians. Blameless life lays the foundation for gracious witness, as Christians *make the most of every opportunity*. The verb literally means 'buying up' or 'buying out': it does not necessarily have the sense (as Eph. 5:16 appears to do) that the time is somehow evil and must be redeemed, but simply that every opportunity is to be snapped up (see O'Brien) like a bargain. The word 'opportunity' may have simply the sense of 'time': the clause is probably an instruction to regard time *as* opportunity for witness, and to use it eagerly as such.

6. This eagerness for witness must not be the excuse for brash arrogance or boring complacency (imagining one's own formulae to contain all the answers). On the contrary: *let your conversation be always full of grace* (the word 'grace' has, in Greek as in English, the possible double meaning of God's grace and human graciousness), *seasoned with salt*. The metaphor of 'salty' speech was a common one in the ancient world. Paul knows that a tedious monologue is worse than useless in evangelism. Christians are to work at making their witness interesting, lively and colourful; and, at the same time, to ensure that they have thoroughly mastered the rudiments of their faith *so that you may know how to answer everyone*. 'Answer' implies that outsiders will ask Christians about their new life, as indeed they will if verse 5 is being obeyed. Many such questions are predictable; but each

[1]For 'outsiders' as a designation of those not within the Christian community see Mk. 4:11; 1 Cor. 5:12–13; 1 Thes. 4:12.

questioner is an individual and must be respected and loved as such. If the 'answer' is heard or felt as an oracular prounncement or a rebuke for ignorance, the argument may be won but the person lost.

Paul's thought has come full circle. Beginning with a report of his thankful prayer for the Colossians (1:3ff.), and of his work for the gospel (1:24 – 2:5), he has ended with the request that they should pray as he prays, and work as he works. Their prayer and life, like his, are to be expressions of the loving wisdom of God, reaching out in Christ to save the world.

IV. FINAL GREETINGS (4:7–18)

Paul concludes with greetings not merely from himself and to the church in general, but from his companions and to various specific people in the church he is addressing. Such closing greetings often tempt scholars to try their hand at reconstructing the jigsaw of historical circumstances, people and movements, that surround the writing of the letters. Many such solutions are fanciful (most of the jigsaw being lost), but some possibilities are at least worth entertaining. It is partly because of this section that one may argue that Paul is writing from prison in Ephesus (see above, pp. 34ff). More importantly, the greetings remind us that we are dealing not with an abstract theological treatise but with a real letter to real people.

The section divides into four short subsections. Paul begins by introducing the bearers of the letter, Tychicus and Onesimus, the former a senior associate of Paul's, the latter perhaps embarrassed to return as a Christian to the town he had fled as a pagan (4:7–9; see Phm. 10). He then conveys greetings from the colleagues who are with him (4:10–14). Third, he sends greetings to Christians in the Colosse area (4:15–17), and finally (4:18) he takes the pen from the secretary and signs his name in a characteristic closing greeting.

A. INTRODUCTION OF MESSENGERS (4:7–9)

7–8. *Tychicus* is acting as Paul's courier on this occasion, but he will do more than merely deposit the letter at Colosse: he *will tell you all the news about me.* What is happening to Paul (see 1:24 – 2:5) is a matter of personal interest and theological concern to the young church. They need to know how it goes with the one who is bearing the torch of the saving purposes of God, partly in order to pray for him (see 4:3, 8) and partly because their life in Christ is bound up mysteriously with him and his work. Tychicus (mentioned in Acts 20:4 as a native of Asia, accompanying Paul on his journey to Jerusalem, and again in 2 Tim. 4:12; Tit. 3:12) is a good choice for a messenger, because *he is a dear brother, a faithful minister and fellow-servant in the Lord.* These three nouns highlight different features of Tychicus' work, not related specifically to any particular 'office' he may have held. 'Brother' means 'fellow-Christian' (as in 1:2); 'minister' (not a semi-technical term as today) refers simply to the fact that Christ works in the church through servants like Tychicus; 'fellow-servant' indicates that, like Paul, Tychicus belongs not to himself but to the Lord. This commendation of Tychicus, his 'note of recommendation' (see 2 Cor. 3:1), conforms to standard practice in the ancient world, and was perhaps particularly necessary when Tychicus was being accompanied by one of whom the Colossian church might be suspicious (4:9). He is 'faithful' (see 1:7), *i.e.* reliable and trustworthy. Paul strongly desires that, through Tychicus, a personal link may be forged between himself and the young church: *I am sending him to you for the express purpose that you may know about our circumstances[1] and that he may encourage your hearts.* These two purposes are not to be separated. As the church hears of Paul's work and concern on their behalf, they will gain fresh strength and confidence. We might compare Philippians 1:12ff. The phrase 'I am sending' is, literally, 'I have sent': Paul projects himself forward in time, and writes as if he is speaking, through the letter, to the Colossian

---

[1]Some MSS read 'that he may know about your circumstances'. This is easily explained as a scribal error. Even though it has the apparent merit of avoiding repetition with vv.7 and 9, it introduces the quite different, and unlikely, idea that Tychicus needed to acquire information about the Colossians. See Metzger, p.626.

church as they hear his words being read.

9. Onesimus, too, has an apostolic commendation. We can reconstruct some of his story from the letter addressed to his master Philemon, which (as we may deduce from this verse) was almost certainly sent at the same time. Tychicus *is coming with Onesimus*, perhaps partly in order to give him moral support and to be there in case further explanations are necessary to convince the Colossians that he too can be styled *our faithful and dear brother*. The church already knows that he *is one of you*, and needs to be assured that he is now this in a deeper sense, not merely a Colossian but also a Christian. Onesimus and Tychicus together *will tell you everything that is happening here*, conveying information not only, perhaps, about Paul, but also about the whole situation of the church in Ephesus (or wherever) and any other local news that might be of interest and importance for the church, perhaps including the possibility of persecution.

B. GREETINGS FROM PAUL'S COMPANIONS (4:10–14)

10–11. Paul now conveys greetings from six colleagues. Of these only *Aristarchus*, a Macedonian from Thessalonica, who in Acts 19:29 is with Paul in Ephesus, and in Acts 20:4 and 27:2 is one of Paul's travelling companions, is described as *my fellow-prisoner*. It may be that the term is metaphorical, Aristarchus being, like Paul, Christ's 'prisoner', but the literal meaning ('fellow-prisoner-of-war') suggests that he, too, is literally imprisoned as Christ's soldier. He *sends you his greetings, as does Mark, the cousin of Barnabas*. Whether or not Mark was the author of the Gospel that bears his name, for which there is no direct evidence in the New Testament itself, we know him as an early member of the Jerusalem church and a relative of some of its more important leaders (Acts 12:12). After his somewhat chequered early career as a missionary (Acts 12:25; 13:13; 15:37–39; *cf.* 2 Tim. 4:11; Phm. 24; 1 Pet. 5:13), Mark is clearly being rehabilitated both as a worker for the gospel and as a companion of Paul. It may be that the following parenthetical command indicates that he had been under a cloud: *you have received* *instructions about him; if he comes to you, welcome him.* Barnabas was of course better known in the early church than Mark (see 1 Cor. 9:6; Gal. 2:1, 9, 13 and Acts 4:36; 9:27; 11:22, 30; 13 – 14 *passim*), and this verse suggests that the rift between him and Paul (Acts 15:36–41, which may or may not be related to that described in Gal. 2:13) was at least in the process of being healed. The mention of Mark's possible visit, especially when coupled with Philemon 22, is an indication that the letter is being written from a location not too far distant from Colosse.

The third greeting comes from *Jesus, who is called Justus,* the only one in the present list of names not to re-appear in Philemon.[1] Together these three, Aristarchus, Mark and Jesus (whose extra name, like those of other early Christians who shared the common Jewish name given to the Lord, serves to distinguish him from his Master), *are the only Jews among my fellow-workers for the kingdom of God.* NIV here follows most commentators, and the passage, read this way, provides the primary evidence for, among other things, the belief that Luke, who is not mentioned until verse 14, was a Gentile. But in the Greek the sentence is not quite so clear. Literally the words mean 'who, being of the circumcision, these ones only (are) fellow-workers for the kingdom of God'. It has been argued that this places the three just named in 'the circumcision party' of Acts 10:45; 11:2; Galatians 2:12. This would (a) allow Luke to be a (Hellenistic?) Jew and (b) indicate a measure of 'ecumenical' co-operation between Paul and those he elsewhere appears to oppose.[2] But in the light of Galatians, and of 2:8–23 of our present letter, it seems difficult to take the phrase 'those . . . of the circumcision' to indicate a party within the church without at the same time expressing Paul's disapproval of it. Perhaps a compromise is possible: Paul may be referring not to a party but to people of a particular background: having belonged to a branch of Christianity more concerned than Paul with observing the Jewish law, they were by now happy to proclaim God's sovereign rule alongside Paul with his different emphases, and as such *they have proved a comfort to me,* showing that not all those

[1]See the commentary on Phm. 23–24.
[2]See E. E. Ellis, *Prophecy and Hermeneutic in Early Christianity: New Testament Essays* (Mohr, 1978), pp.116–128.

who were on the opposing 'side' in Galatians 2:11ff. were inflexibly opposed to him. But the point should not be over-stressed; NIV may well be right. It is, incidentally, only in this passage that we learn that Aristarchus (see above) is Jewish.

12–13. It was *Epaphras* who originally preached the gospel in Colosse, and brought the news to Paul that there was now a church there (1:7–8). He, like Onesimus, *is one of you, i.e.* he is himself from Colosse, and had presumably become *a servant of Christ Jesus* in Ephesus under Paul's ministry. He too now *sends greetings*. He does more: *he is always*, like Paul himself (1:29 – 2:3), *wrestling in prayer for you, that you may stand firm, mature and fully assured in all the will of God*. NIV has altered the order of the words, making 'mature and fully assured' come at the end of the sentence; in the Greek, however, it precedes, and is closely connected with, the phrase 'in all the will of God'. God's 'will' is not restricted to the question 'what does God want the Colossian Christians to do?', but is a larger entity, as we see from 1:24 – 2:5 and especially Ephesians 1:5–12. It refers to God's whole strategy for the salvation of the world. Epaphras is praying (like Paul) that the young church will understand what it is that God is doing and order their lives accordingly, growing into well-grounded Christian (and human) maturity. As is clear from 1:3–12 and 2:1–3, Paul regards prayer as more than just a pious ancillary activity to preaching and teaching: it is part of the work itself. *I vouch for him that he is working hard for you and for those at Laodicea*, a few miles down the road, *and Hierapolis*, a little to the north of Laodicea. Though not physically present there, Epaphras has a vision for God's work in the Lycus valley, and is working hard to bring it to reality.

14. The last two *greetings* are from *our dear friend Luke, the doctor, and Demas*. It is only in this passage that we learn of Luke's profession, and only by inference, and later tradition, that we know him as the author of the great two-volume work which comprises the Gospel named after him and the Acts of the Apostles.[1] It is, none the less, noteworthy that Paul has as

[1]See I. H. Marshall, *The Gospel of Luke: A Commentary on the Greek Text* (Paternoster, 1978), pp.33–35. For the question of whether Luke was with Paul in Ephesus see above, p.36.

companions two of those to whom tradition, and a reasonable cross-section of scholarship, have ascribed the writing of Gospels. Luke is also listed among the greetings in Philemon 24. In 2 Timothy 4:11 he is Paul's only companion, Demas having departed (2 Tim. 4:10) 'because he loved this world' – a sad but cryptic allusion to a desertion about which we have no other information.

C. GREETINGS TO CHRISTIANS IN THE COLOSSE AREA (4:15–17)

15. Paul does not often greet by name individual Christians in the churches to which he writes. The main exception to this is Romans (16:3–16), the one other letter, perhaps significantly, written to a church which Paul had not visited in person. He seems to be taking care to establish relationships with those he has not met. So he writes *Give my greetings to the brothers* (*i.e.* the church) *at Laodicea, and to Nympha and the church in her house.* Much ink has been spilt over the question whether the individual here mentioned (who seems to be part of the church in Laodicea, though that is not absolutely certain) is a woman (Nympha) or a man (Nymphas). Both forms are found in the manuscript tradition, and certainty seems impossible on this (fortunately not very significant) point. What is evident is that the church, possessing as yet no 'special' buildings of its own, would meet in private houses. The group might be large or small: the early church felt itself under no obligation, as did the synagogue, to ensure a quorum of worshippers (see Mt. 18:20).

16. The next two verses set further puzzles for the historian. *After this letter has been read to you, see that it is also read in the church of the Laodiceans and that you in turn read the letter from Laodicea.* It is clear from this that Paul intends his letters to be read out in the assembled church and thus to function as authoritative. This is apparent already in 1:24 – 2:5, and further illustrations of the same point are found in 1 Thessalonians 5:27 and Philemon 2. Here we undoubtedly have the principal reason for the preservation of Paul's letters in the sub-apostolic period, and their eventual adoption as part of the canonical 'new covenant' books: their author intended them to carry, in writing, the authority which had been invested in him as an apostle. His work as a whole was to lay foundations for the new world-wide people of God (1 Cor. 3:10–11; Eph. 2:20), and his letters were designed to function, and did in fact function, as part of the fulfilment of that commission. Colossians is itself a good example, being intended to ensure that the young church was truly founded on Christ himself. And if this is the reason why (apart from their intrinsic worth) Paul's letters were kept, this verse also indicates something of how the process of collecting them together was at least begun. This letter, sent to Colosse, is to be (copied? and) passed on to the church in Laodicea; the Laodiceans, who have also received a letter, are to pass theirs on to Colosse, perhaps by having Tychicus bring it with him (he would almost certainly pass through Laodicea on his way to Colosse).

But what of this second letter, the one 'from Laodicea'? Most scholars now agree that this phrase does not indicate a letter written (to Paul? or to the Colossians?) by the Laodicean churches, but rather one written *to* Laodicea and now to be passed on *from* Laodicea to Colosse. The almost overwhelming probability is that it was written by Paul himself.[1] But what did it consist of? Lightfoot's discussion of the matter[2] remains standard. He argues that the 'letter from Laodicea' is none other than (what we call) Ephesians, which shows itself to be a circular by the absence of specific greetings and of advice directed to particular situations, by the lack (in many MSS) of an address, and by the general, wide-ranging tone that prevails throughout. This suggestion has not been widely accepted by scholars (Caird is an exception). But no major arguments have been specifically advanced against it, and it may be worth while to outline its implications further in terms of a hypothetical reconstruction of events. According to this possibility, Paul, in prison at Ephesus,

[1]Despite C. P. Anderson, 'Who Wrote "The Epistle from Laodicea"?', *JBL* 85, 1966, pp.436–440, who argues for Epaphras. The discussion below will indicate why I think his theory unnecessary.

[2]Lightfoot, pp.274–300, including a full discussion of the clearly spurious 'Letter to the Laodiceans', a forgery well known in the Patristic period and subsequently. See also Lightfoot's article on 'The Destination of the Epistle to the Ephesians' in his *Biblical Essays* (Macmillan, 1893), pp.375–396.

wrote 'Ephesians' as a general letter to the young churches in the surrounding area, including no doubt the church in Ephesus itself. Tychicus (Eph. 6:21) was despatched with the copy for the churches in the Lycus valley area, with the intention of visiting Colosse after Laodicea, as would be natural (see the map on p. 17). But Paul does not want the Colossian church to be merely another recipient of a circular, any more than he had wanted to include in that majestic and poetic 'circular' the more specific warnings of Colossians 2, relevant though they will be for Laodicea also. So Tychicus takes with him 'Ephesians', Colossians, and – Onesimus; the latter bearing the shorter letter intended for his erstwhile master Philemon.

This hypothesis is, of course, unprovable. But (in my judgment at least) it covers the data well, particularly the close relationship between 'Ephesians' and Colossians. 'Ephesians' may be seen as the result of the author taking a step back, as it were, from Colossians and contemplating in worship the great truths he has been emphasizing. (Conversely, of course, Colossians could be seen as a more sharply focused version of certain themes in 'Ephesians'.) But even if this detailed reconstruction is not accepted, and if (with most scholars) we consider the 'letter to Laodicea' long since lost, the underlying point of the verse remains clear. The authority which Paul has been given to build up the churches in the faith is to be exercised by the two letters to the Lycus valley being read out in both Laodicea and Colosse.

17. The most cryptic comment comes last: *Tell Archippus* (who in Phm. 2 is described as Paul's 'fellow-soldier', and seems to be a member of Philemon's household, or at least his house-church): '*See to it that you complete the work you have received in the Lord.*' It is possible that the 'work' (literally, 'ministry'; see below) is the specific task of acceding to Paul's request concerning Onesimus. But there are problems with this view, which we will discuss in the introduction to Philemon. Much more likely is the view that Archippus has been set aside for a particular ministry within the congregation, perhaps that of teaching the young converts, building them up in faith and love. If he had (to use Paul's metaphor) already seen active service in the company of the apostle himself, he would be well fitted for this task. This would cohere with the language used of Paul himself in 1:25, where the verb used for 'present . . . in fullness' is the same as that used here for 'complete'. Paul's desire throughout the letter has been that the Colossian church should grow to maturity, and it is likely that this final instruction would relate to that process. Archippus has received a 'ministry' (not a specific office, but a specifically Christian task) 'in the Lord': he is to find *his* fulfilment in being the Lord's agent to bring the church to *its* fulfilment.

D. SIGNATURE OF THE APOSTLE (4:18)

Just as, today, someone who dictates a letter to a secretary will usually sign it in person, so here and in several other letters (1 Cor. 16:21; Gal. 6:11; 2 Thes. 3:17; *cf.* Phm. 19) we find that *Paul* likes to take the pen from the secretary (see Rom. 16:22) and *write this greeting in my own hand*, as a mark of both authentication and affection. He has bound the young church to himself in prayer and loving concern, and now makes his final appeal to them, and to the Lord on their behalf: *Remember my chains. Grace be with you.* The first sentence is as much a reminder of his paradoxical authority (see Phm. 9) as an appeal for prayer support, though it is pretty certainly that as well (see Eph. 6:20, which echoes the present verse and Phm. 9). The second is another example of a conventional formula charged with rich meaning. From one point of view, grace has been the subject of the whole letter. Paul has written in order to emphasize the undeserved love of God in Christ, and all that follows from it. From another point of view, grace has been the *object* of the letter: Paul has written in order to be a *means* of grace, not merely to describe it. The letter closes as it began, in grateful prayer.

As we look back over what Paul has written to the Christians in Colosse, we get a glimpse of the young church in its daily life: worshipping, encouraging one another, learning more fully of the plan of God for the world's salvation and of their place in that plan, finding out how to fulfil, as individuals and as a community, the ministries they have received in the Lord, and, above all, discovering how to be truly grateful to God and so to advance to maturity as Christians and as human beings.

> Wherefore I cry, and cry again;
> And in no quiet canst thou be,
> Till I a thankful heart obtain
> Of thee:
>
> Not thankful, when it pleaseth me;
> As if thy blessings had spare days:
> But such a heart, whose pulse may be
> Thy praise.[1]

We see, also, an attractive picture of Paul, battling in prayer on behalf of Christians he has never met, tactfully introducing himself and his work to them. His breath-taking vision of what God is doing in the world forms a strange, yet strangely characteristic, contrast with the circumstances out of which he writes. But when we look at the church and the apostle in this way, we see more: the loving wisdom of God, the wise plan of salvation now become flesh and blood, the new Adam ushering in the new Age in which men, women and children of all races are bidden, and enabled, to worship the one true God. Paul's ministry is 'in Christ', and reflects Christ at every point. The young church has come to fullness of life in him. All that Paul has said to the Colossians amounts to a royal invitation to adoration, gratitude and love. God has, in Christ, reconciled to himself the world he created through Christ, and now invites his people to enjoy that reconciliation, to grow up into the full and rich human life of the new Age, and so to enjoy him. By beholding Christ, the image of God, they are to be changed into his likeness.

---

[1]George Herbert, 'Gratefulness'.

PHILEMON:
INTRODUCTION

I. THE CIRCUMSTANCES OF WRITING

Although the letter to Philemon is the shortest of Paul's sur-
viving letters, it is longer than most secular letters from the same
period. It is no mere casual note, but a carefully crafted and
sensitively worded piece, employing tact and irony. There is no
doubt that Paul himself wrote it.

But why did he write it? In particular, to whom is he really
speaking, and what is he asking for? Philemon appears to be the
addressee (v.1). But a case has been made for a different view:
that Philemon, a resident not of Colosse but of Laodicea, was
the overseer of all the Lycus valley churches, and that he merely
had the task of handing the letter on to Archippus (v.2), who
was the actual owner of Onesimus, and in whose house the
Colossian church, or part of it, met (v.2). The 'letter from
Laodicea' which is to be read in Colosse (Col. 4:16) is (on this
view) our 'Philemon'; the 'ministry' which Archippus is to fulfil
(Col. 4:17) is his acceding to Paul's request concerning
Onesimus, his slave. John Knox, the scholar who pioneered this
alternative view of our epistle,[1] coupled it with the suggestion of
E. J. Goodspeed that the letter was preserved because, despite
its personal and apparently non-theological nature, it meant a
great deal to the first collector of the Pauline letters, namely
Onesimus himself, the Bishop of Ephesus referred to by
Ignatius in his own letter to the Ephesians, 1:3 (dated around AD

[1]John Knox, *Philemon Among the Letters of Paul: A New View of Its Place and Importance*, rev.
edn. (Abingdon, 1959: 1st edn. 1935); see too Goodspeed, *An Introduction to the New
Testament* (Chicago U.P., 1937), pp.109–124.

110–115).

Goodspeed's theory can be neither proved nor disproved. It is possible: but is it probable? Onesimus' early training with Paul might well have meant that a young slave of AD 55 (or 60–62, if the letter is written from Rome) might have become a respected senior churchman by AD 115. But the name 'Onesimus' was not uncommon, and the echoes of this letter in that of Ignatius are mostly very tenuous. Nor is there any evidence that Onesimus – either the slave, or the bishop – was the collector of the Pauline corpus. Even if Ephesians was designed to stand at the head of the set, that would prove nothing. Goodspeed might be right, but might equally well be wrong, and little of historical or theological importance attaches to the decision.

Knox's more radical hypothesis (that Archippus is the real addressee) has, however, been shown several times to create more problems than it solves.[1] (a) I have suggested in the commentary on Colossians 4:16–17 that there is a more natural way of taking those verses. (b) Though it is true that 'Philemon' is addressed formally to a church fellowship as well as to an individual, and that the addressee is spoken to as a member of the Christian community, the body of the letter reads as a one-to-one appeal – hardly designed to be read aloud to the assembled faithful in both Laodicea and Colosse. (c) The fact that it is Archippus' name that, in verse 2, immediately precedes the mention of the church 'in your (singular) house', does not at all prove that Archippus is the leader of the church or the real addressee. Parallels from other ancient letters which begin with more than one greeting[2] show that it is the first name that indicates the person for whom the letter is primarily intended. We may therefore safely take it that the letter is being written by Paul, in prison (probably in Ephesus, in which case the action takes place in the early to middle fifties of the first century), to Philemon, who lived, and had the oversight of a house-church, in Colosse. Tychicus and Onesimus are taking with them not

---

[1] It is criticized in damaging detail by, e.g., Moule, Caird, O'Brien, Stuhlmacher and Bruce, Paul, pp.401 ff. At the time of going to press a further 'new look' on Philemon is being suggested by S. B. C. Winter: see 'Methodological Observations on a New Interpretation of Paul's Letter to Philemon' in Union Seminary Quarterly Review 39, 1984, pp.203–212.

[2] See Lohse, pp.190 f.

only the main Colossian letter (Col. 4:7–9) but also this more personal note to one of the church's leaders.

II. THE NATURE OF THE REQUEST

But what was Paul asking Philemon to do? Here the matter becomes surprisingly complicated. From the letter itself it appears that Onesimus had run away from Philemon's household, perhaps taking some money as he went (see the notes on v.18). This would not be unusual in the ancient world. Many slaves risked the wrath of their owners (backed up by stringent laws) in the attempt to escape.

At this point Onesimus could have joined a band of other ex-slaves, hidden himself in the underworld of a big city, or fled for refuge to a pagan shrine.[1] Instead, whether by design or sheer providence, he had met Paul. And he had become a Christian.

Paul was now in a delicate position. Our knowledge of the slave-laws then obtaining in the province of Asia is insufficient to tell us what his legal position would have been (see Stuhlmacher, pp.23f.), but harbouring a runaway slave was hardly the sort of behaviour to earn Paul a good reputation or to help him regain his own freedom (v.22). Anyway, more than legality was at stake. Paul was faced with two estranged Christians, both of whom, under God, owed their salvation to him (v.19). But if the gospel both have embraced is the message of reconciliation (Col. 1:18–20; 3:12–17; *cf.* 2 Cor. 5:17–21), then it must be able to bring together slave and free as it did Jew and Greek, or male and female (Col. 3:11; Gal. 3:28). Paul is faced with a test case. It is no use preaching grand-sounding theory if it cannot be put into practice when it is needed. So he sends Onesimus back to Colosse, to Philemon, having done his best, in this letter, to ensure that a full reconciliation will take place.

But is their reconciliation Paul's main aim? It has been suggested that the real purpose of the letter was to ask Philemon to send Onesimus back to Paul. Thus verses 13–14 say that, though

[1] See Stuhlmacher, pp.22 f., for these and other options open to a runaway slave.

Paul would like to keep Onesimus, he prefers only to act with Philemon's consent.[1] But there are four problems with this view.

First, it leaves little room for verse 21 ('knowing that you will do even more than I ask'). This must mean that Paul is (a) making an initial request and (b) hinting at a further, unspecified favour. But if the initial request is for Onesimus to be given permanently to Paul, what 'more' could there be?

Second, verse 15 strongly suggests that Onesimus and Philemon are at least to be prepared to live together again. If this is the basic request, the 'something more' may be a delicate hint that Philemon, having been fully reconciled to Onesimus, might consider either giving him his freedom or perhaps (which would amount to the same thing) 'lending' him permanently to Paul as a helper and travelling companion.

Third, the weight of argument throughout falls not on Onesimus' possible future service to Paul but on the reconciliation that Paul wishes to take place. The actual imperatives all point this way: welcome him (v.17), put down any offences to my account (v.18), and so refresh my heart (v.20); and prepare a guest room for me (v.22).

Fourth, the arguments supporting this appeal likewise point to reconciliation as the main aim. An important parallel, and contrast, is provided by the superficially similar letter of the younger Pliny to his friend Sabinianus, whose freedman (one degree above a slave) had come to Pliny for help (*Ep.* 9:21). Pliny appeals to self-interest ('mercy wins most praise when there was just cause for anger . . . anger can only be a torment to your gentle self') and sides with Sabinianus against the hapless freedman ('I have given the man a very severe scolding and warned him firmly that I will never make such a request again'). The request is not for a full-hearted reconciliation, but for 'some concession to his youth, his tears, and your own kind heart'.[2]

---

[1]Houlden (pp.225 f.) suggests that Onesimus had not run away at all, but had been loaned to Paul in the first place, making v.18 refer to a small matter over which Philemon was unnecessarily offended. (See now also Winter, as in n.1, p.165, above.) But the whole letter implies a more serious breach.

[2]The translation is taken from Betty Radice, *The Letters of the Younger Pliny* (Penguin, 1963), p.246. A subsequent letter (9:24; in *ibid.*, p.248) shows that the request was granted.

Paul's motivation, and appeal, are entirely different (this provides the answer to those early Fathers who thought the book untheological and unworthy of an apostle).[1] Paul is not asking for a paternalistic willingness to let bygones be bygones. Nor is he offering good advice to Philemon on how to maintain a dignified detachment, untroubled by passion or anger. He seeks the specifically Christian virtue of loving forgiveness, which will demand humility from both parties – Onesimus to seek forgiveness, Philemon to grant it. Onesimus must abandon fear: Philemon, pride.[2] And the thing which will induce both parties to do this is a theological fact, namely the fellowship (koinōinia) which belongs to the people of Christ.

If, then, Christian reconciliation is Paul's aim, the driving force of the whole letter is the prayer of verse 6, which, though cryptically expressed, is comprehensible in the light of the letter as a whole (see the notes for details). Philemon is to learn in practice that koinōnia means an 'interchange' between those who are Christ's.[3] Paul first identifies himself closely with Philemon (vv. 1–7): then he establishes the closest possible ties between himself and Onesimus (vv. 10–14). The result of this 'interchange' is that Onesimus and Philemon are brought together – in Paul (vv. 17–20). As Luther saw,[4] Paul plays Christ in the drama, identifying himself with both sinner and offended party, so making peace (cf. 2 Cor. 5:16–21, which contains many theological ideas here put into practical effect). The result is that the church, instead of fragmenting, grows together 'into Christ' (v.6). There will always be forces that try to tear the church apart. But there will always be the gospel itself to point the way – of humility, forgiveness and reconciliation – by which unity can be not only precariously preserved but solidly established.

Why did Paul not simply ask for Onesimus to be released from slavery? Why (for that matter) did he not order all Christian

---

[1]See Lightfoot, pp.316 f.

[2]See the notes on Col. 3:5 ff., above. I have explored this aspect of the letter more fully in ch. 11 of my book *Small Faith – Great God* (Kingsway, 1978).

[3]See M. D. Hooker, 'Interchange in Christ', *JTS* n.s. 22, 1971, pp.349–361, esp. 360–361. For the theory that this *koinōnia* is based at least in part on the Roman idea of *societas*, 'partnership', see J. P. Sampley, *Pauline Partnership in Christ: Christian Community and Commitment in Light of Roman Law* (Fortress, 1980), discussed briefly in n.1, p.176, below.

[4]See Lohse, p.188, quoting from Luther's Preface to Philemon.

slave-owners to release all their slaves, rather than profit from an unjust social structure? Slavery was one of the really great evils of the ancient world, under which a large proportion of the population belonged totally to another person, for better or (usually) for worse, with no rights, no prospects, the possibility of sexual abuse, the chance of torture or death for trivial offences. Some slaves were fortunate in having kind or generous masters, and by the end of the first century some secular writers were expressing disgust at the institution. But for the great majority, life was at best drudgery and at worst 'merciless exploitation'.[1] Why, then, did Paul not protest against the whole dehumanizing system?

What alternatives were actually open to him? He was committed to the life, and the standards, of the new age over against the old (Col. 3). But a loud protest, at that moment in social history, would have functioned simply on the level of the old age: it would have been heard only as a criticism by one part of society (Paul, not himself a slave-owner, had nothing to lose) against another. It would, without a doubt, have done more harm than good, making life harder for Christian slaves, and drawing upon the young church exactly the wrong sort of attention from the authorities. If Paul is jailed for proclaiming 'another king' (Acts 17:7), it must be clear that the kingdom in question is of a different order altogether from that of Caesar. In addition, inveighing against slavery *per se* would have been totally ineffective: one might as well, in modern Western society, protest against the mortgage system. Even if all Christians of Paul's day were suddenly to release their slaves, it is by no means clear that the slaves themselves, or society in general, would benefit: a large body of people suddenly unemployed in the ancient world might not enjoy their freedom as much as they would imagine.

Paul's method is subtler. He of course knows (1 Cor. 7:21-23) that in principle it is better to be free than to be a slave. But, like Jesus, his way of changing the world is to plant a grain of mustard seed, which, inconspicuous at first, grows into a

---

[1]R. H. Barrow, in *OCD*, *s.v.* On ancient slavery in general, in addition to that article, see Lightfoot, pp.319-323, and now H. Koester, *Introduction to the New Testament*, vol. 1, pp.59-62 (with bibliography), 330-332.

spreading tree. And in the meantime (see the commentary on Col. 3:22 – 4:1) he teaches slaves and masters to treat themselves, and each other, as human beings. Like the artist or poet, he does some of his finest work not by the obscure clarity of direct statement, but by veiled allusion and teasing suggestion.

III. THE PLACE OF PHILEMON IN THE NEW TESTAMENT

Why was the letter preserved? We cannot tell. Philemon himself may have treasured it. Onesimus may have kept a copy, and if indeed it is he to whom Ignatius later refers as Bishop of Ephesus, it is quite likely that 'his' letter would have been preserved, with others, in that city. Of one thing we may be sure. It is unlikely that the letter would have been preserved if it had not been received in the spirit in which it was sent. We are on safe ground in postulating a happy ending to the story. The reconciliation of Philemon and Onesimus becomes an acted parable of the gospel itself, which breaks into the world of sin, suspicion and anger, of pride and fear, with the good news that Jesus Christ has revealed God's purposes of salvation, of human wholeness, of loving and forgiving fellowship.

The letter to Philemon appears to pose in a peculiarly acute form the problem of hermeneutics – of how we, today, can appropriate this part of Scripture for ourselves. This letter was written to a private individual in a unique situation in the life of his household. But no part of the New Testament more clearly demonstrates integrated Christian thinking and living. It offers a blend, utterly characteristic of Paul, of love, wisdom, humour, gentleness, tact and above all Christian and human maturity. The epistle's chief value is not that it is a tract about slavery, for it is not that. It is a letter which, at one level 'about' *koinōnia*, Christian fellowship and mutual participation, is at a far deeper level an outworking, in practice, of that principle. That which it expounds, it also exemplifies. It is a living fragment of the life of Christ, working itself out in the lives of human beings so different from us and yet so similar. Perhaps the only hermeneutical principle we need here is the crisp command, issued in another context where custom and faith were in collision: go, and do thou likewise.

IV. THE OUTLINE OF THE LETTER

There is no problem about the analysis of this letter into its component parts, except that which we noticed about Colossians: Paul's thought does not move in neat, packaged sections, but grows and develops from pregnant statements (here, vv.4–7) to fuller exposition (vv.8–22). We arrive at the following outline:

I. OPENING GREETINGS (1–3)

II. THANKSGIVING AND PRAYER (4–7)

III. THE REQUEST (8–22)

    A. ONESIMUS AND PAUL (8–16)
    B. ONESIMUS AND PHILEMON (17–22)

IV. CLOSING GREETINGS (23–25)

PHILEMON: COMMENTARY

I. OPENING GREETINGS (1-3)

1. Nowhere else does *Paul* open a letter by referring to himself as *a prisoner of Christ Jesus*. Putting aside the mention of rank ('apostle', Gal. 1:1; see vv.8–9) or task ('servant', Rom. 1:1), he faces Philemon with his current imprisonment, which will form a sub-theme of the whole letter (vv.9–10, 13, 22–23). Otherwise the opening follows the usual pattern (see on Col. 1:1–2). *Timothy our brother* is with Paul. It is never said that he too is a prisoner. Despite this formal mention of Timothy, the letter as a whole is clearly a very personal one from Paul himself, not a joint effort.

It is addressed primarily *to Philemon*[1] *our dear friend and fellow-worker*. These epithets imply that he, unlike most of the Colossian church (Col. 2:1), has known Paul personally, and has collaborated with him in the work of the gospel – unless 'fellow-worker' is simply an acknowledgment that his work for Christ makes him automatically a colleague, albeit at a distance. Philemon had himself been converted through the ministry of Paul (v.19): probably during a visit to Ephesus, though some have speculated that the two met while Paul was on his journey 'through the interior' from the region of Galatia and Phrygia to Ephesus (Acts 18:23; 19:1; see the map on p.17).

2. If Onesimus is to be welcomed back, it must be by the entire household. Paul therefore writes also *to Apphia our sister*,

---

[1]A not uncommon name: see Lightfoot, pp.303–306.

who is almost universally reckoned to be Philemon's wife,[1] and
herself a Christian ('sister'), and *to Archippus our fellow-soldier*,
who, cryptically addressed in Colossians 4:17 (see Introduction,
pp.164f.), is, like Philemon, a partner in Paul's work. He shares
his particular title, which the NEB renders 'comrade-in-arms',
with Epaphroditus (Phil. 2:25). On the theory that he was the
real addressee of the letter, see the Introduction.

The letter is personal, but nobody is an island: *and to the church
that meets in your home*. Philemon's life is set in a corporate
Christian context. The early church, having no 'special' buildings of its own, met in private houses.[2] Philemon's house-
church may have comprised the entire Colossian Christian community, though there may well have been others, perhaps
including that of Nympha(s) (see on Col. 4:15). The church in
Rome probably consisted of several such groups (see Rom. 16:5,
10, 11, 14, 15), and part of the reason for Paul's appeals for unity
may stem from the risk of fragmentation thus created. Here his
main concern is for the internal unity of Philemon's house-
church as its members contemplate the return, as a brother in
Christ, of a slave about whom they had at the very least mixed
feelings.

3. To meet this (and every) challenge to their faith and love,
Philemon and his household will require more than merely
human qualities. They will need *Grace . . . and peace from God our
Father and the Lord Jesus Christ*. This conventional greeting (see
on Col. 1:2) never becomes merely a pious phrase or throw-
away remark. Paul wants his letters to be a means of grace – that
is why he writes – and he intends them to result in peace, the
rich harmony of human beings with God and with one another.
This can come about only if God himself gives these Christ-
shaped gifts to his people.

[1]She could of course be his mother, sister or other female relative. For the form and
background of the name see the very full note in Lightfoot, pp.306–308.
[2]These house-churches have been the subject of a good deal of study in recent years: see
the excursus in Stuhlmacher, pp.70–75, and, on the overall social context, E. A. Judge, *The
Social Pattern of Christian Groups in the First Century* (Tyndale Press, 1960) and now W. A.
Meeks, *The First Urban Christians: The Social World of the Apostle Paul* (Yale University Press,
1983), pp.74–110.

II. THANKSGIVING AND PRAYER (4–7)

As in Colossians 1:3ff., Paul follows contemporary style in telling his readers that he is praying for them: and his prayers usually focus on thanksgiving. What God *has* done for the addressees is the basis of what he *will* do for them, including what he will do through their reading of this letter. Thus we find numerous echoes of verses 4–7 in the rest of the letter: 'love' in verses 5, 9; 'fellowship' (*i.e.* the *koinōnia* root) in verses 6, 17; 'good' in verses 6, 14; 'heart' (*splangchna*, literally 'entrails', 'bowels') in verses 7, 12 and 20; 'refresh' in verses 7, 20 and 'brother' also in verses 7, 20. All of these lead us to expect that the prayer Paul records in verses 4–7 will be the basis for the appeal of verses 8–20, and so it proves to be.

4–5. Philemon can be assured that Paul is not seeking his own ends, but God's best will for him, since *I always thank my God as I remember you in my prayers*. To refer to God as 'my God' evokes the Psalms (*cf.* Pss. 3:7; 5:2; 7:1, 3; 18:2, 6; 22:1; 42:6, 11; 43:4, 5, *etc.*). The 'always' could go with the thanksgiving, as in NIV, RSV, NEB (*i.e.* whenever Paul prays for Philemon, he gives thanks to God) or with the remembering, as in JB ('I always mention you in my prayers and thank God for you'), AV, *etc.* It matters little: even in the first, Paul does not imply that his prayers are haphazard. More important is the content of his thanksgiving: *because I hear about your faith in the Lord Jesus and your love for all the saints*. The Greek original of this clause presents a problem, since literally it reads 'hearing of your love and faith which you have towards the Lord Jesus and to all the saints' (see RSV). It is possible that both the love and the faith are directed towards both Jesus and other Christians, but to take it this way involves understanding 'faith' in two different ways, first as 'trust in' and secondly as 'faithfulness towards'. Better to read it as a literary pattern in which the first and fourth elements, and the second and third, are matched up (AB : BA);[1] *i.e.* taking A with A (love . . . to the other

---

[1]See the brief discussion of this literary device in BDF, p.477.

Christians) and B with B (faith towards Jesus Christ). (Notice the difference between 'towards' and 'to', *pros* and *eis*, in the original.) This leads us back to the NIV translation of the verse. It is difficult to say whether Paul would have constructed this literary device deliberately, or whether his thought ran on too fast for his words, so that, in stating the reason for Philemon's love (his faith in the Lord Jesus), he omitted to mention the object of that love until afterwards. This love and faith are not there by accident, but are the result of a gracious work of God. Paul mentions love first, no doubt because it is to love that he will appeal. But, as we shall see, underneath this love at every point is Christ, seen by faith.

6. The next verse expresses the content of Paul's prayer for Philemon (as opposed to further reasons for thanksgiving, to which Paul appears to return in v.7). NIV's *I pray that* has been added to the verse to make this clear. But that is virtually the only thing scholars have been able to agree on about this verse. Every element in it seems to throw another set of questions at the modern reader. What precisely is Paul praying *for*? I have discussed the verse in more detail elsewhere,[1] and here summarize the conclusions reached there.

The clue to the verse lies both in the fact that it is related to the rest of the epistle as premise to conclusion – *i.e.* the prayer undergirds the appeal – and, more particularly, in the theological nature of that appeal. As I suggested in the Introduction, Paul's argument is based on what has been called 'interchange', that mutuality of Christian life which, springing from common participation in the body of Christ, extends beyond mere common concern into actual exchange: 'if we are distressed, it is for your comfort and salvation . . . because we know that just as you share in our sufferings, so also you share in our comfort' (2 Cor. 1:6–7, with which compare 4:10–15 and of course Col. 1:24). Philemon is to welcome Onesimus as if he were Paul, and to debit Paul's bill as if *he* were Onesimus (vv.17–19). The Greek word that says all this is *koinōnia*,[2] and that is the key to verse 6.

[1]See my article on Phm. 5, forthcoming in *JSNT*.   [2]See 2 Cor. 1:7; Phil. 2:1–5; 3:10.

This Greek word *koinōnia* is difficult to translate. 'Fellowship' means, for many, simply the enjoyment of the company of other Christians: 'sharing' usually implies mutual giving and receiving of material things; 'interchange' itself, useful for highlighting the way *koinōnia* functions, seems a bit mechanical. The idea we need to grasp – the theme that dominates the letter – is that, in Christ, Christians not only belong to one another but actually become mutually identified, truly rejoicing with the happy and genuinely weeping with the sad (Rom. 12:15; *cf.* 1 Cor. 12:26; 2 Cor. 11:28–29). *Koinōnia* is part of the truth about the body of Christ. All are bound together in a mutual bond that makes our much-prized individualism look shallow and petty. This fundamental meaning of *koinōnia* best explains its other uses, particularly that of 'generosity' or 'almsgiving' (*e.g.* Rom. 15:26; 2 Cor. 8:4): Christians give to one another because they belong to one another. NIV, which here reads *that you may be active in sharing your faith,* introduces a quite extraneous idea, since the phrase 'sharing your faith' is used today to refer to conversational evangelism, which, though important, is not what Paul is talking about. *Koinōnia* cannot mean 'sharing' in the sense of dividing something up or parcelling it out. Nor is it the language primarily of business.[1] The key idea is 'mutual participation'. The whole phrase then means 'the mutual participation which is proper to your faith'. The faith is referred to as Philemon's, not because it is different to anybody else's (it is simply faith in Jesus Christ: that, as we will see, is the whole point), but simply because it is he to whom the appeal is being made.

The rest of the sentence then begins to fall into place. Paul prays that the fact of this mutual participation will 'work powerfully' within Philemon[2] to produce 'knowledge'. This 'knowledge' is not merely theoretical understanding but an integrated and operational grasp of 'every good thing', *i.e.* what God is doing in Christ and what he, Philemon, must do in conse-

---

[1] So O'Brien, p.280. Though there are some significant parallels between Paul's idea of 'fellowship' and the idea of *societas*, 'partnership', in the Roman world (see Sampley, *Pauline Partnership*), what we have here goes beyond this. Sampley notes (pp.79–81) the presence in Phm. 17 of the *societas* motif, but he does not see that this is based on the Christian *koinōnia* expressed in v.6. See below.
[2] See the parallels in Eph. 1:17; Phil. 1:9; Col. 1:9–10.

quence. It is related to 'good' in verse 14: 'something which is *done* or *performed* . . ., rather than a *possession* or the *object of knowledge*'.[1] If Philemon allows the principle of mutual participation (itself part of his faith in Christ) powerfully to inform his thinking and living, then the right results will follow.

This understanding of the first half of the verse leads, finally, to a satisfactory solution for the last four words (literally: 'in us unto Christ'). Most translations give up the attempt to maintain Paul's exact wording: NIV *we have in Christ* is typical of many. We should probably supply a repetition of the 'power' root, perhaps a verb ('work powerfully'), to indicate that it is God who is accomplishing these things in his people.[2] 'In us' in our present context evokes the idea of God's being at work in his people to produce the conduct which will delight him.

This leaves the apparently awkward phrase 'unto Christ'. Some have suggested taking the phrase to refer to the second coming of Christ, or to mean 'for the glory of Christ', but neither of these really fits.[3] I believe, rather, that 'unto Christ' is best taken in the sense of Ephesians 4:12–13, 'so that the body of Christ may be built up until we all reach unity in the faith and in the knowledge of the Son of God and become mature, *attaining to the whole measure of the fulness of Christ*'.[4]

I suggest, in other words, that Paul uses 'Christ' here, as in some other passages,[5] as a shorthand for the full and mature life of those 'in Christ', so that 'unto Christ' refers to the growth of the church towards that goal. Paul's desire is that the fact of mutual participation, enjoyed by Philemon and his fellow Christians, will result in the full blessing of being 'in Christ', *i.e.* the full unity of the body of Christ: referring specifically in this case to the reconciliation of slave and master (*cf.* Gal. 3:28).

The verse as a whole, then, could be paraphrased as follows: 'I am praying that the mutual participation which is proper to the Christian faith you hold may have its full effect in your realization of every good thing that God wants to accomplish in

[1]Moule, p.143: italics original.
[2]See 1 Cor. 12:6; 2 Cor. 4:12; Gal. 3:5; Eph. 3:20; Phil. 2:13; Col. 1:29; 1 Thes. 2:13.
[3]For these and other options, see O'Brien, p.281.   [4]See too Eph. 1:23.
[5]E.g. Gal. 3:16 (on which see E. E. Ellis, *Paul's Use of the Old Testament* (Oliver and Boyd, 1957), pp.70 ff.); 4:19; 1 Cor. 1:13; 12:12.

us to lead us into the fullness of Christian fellowship, that is, of Christ.' To read the verse in this way does justice to the apparent peculiarities of what Paul has actually written, imports no ideas extraneous to the epistle, and prepares the way exactly and thoroughly for the appeal that is to come.

7. From this vantage-point we can see that verse 7 explains verse 6 as well as verse 5. (NIV, following most scholars, implicitly links v.7 to v.5 only, omitting the 'for' which joins vv.6 and 7.) The reason why Paul has confidence in praying like this for Philemon is that he knows he is building on strength: for *your love has given me great joy and encouragement, because you, brother, have refreshed the hearts of the saints.* As in Colossians 1:8, it is love that gives Paul the greatest encouragement, because it is the surest sign that Christ is being formed in his people. Philemon's love means that the church in Colosse experiences Christ's love not only directly, in personal communion with him, but also through their leader: their 'hearts' (literally 'entrails': the word is used frequently to indicate the seat of the deepest emotions) have been 'refreshed' through him. The verb here is in origin a military metaphor, signifying the rest that an army takes while on the march. The Colossian Christians, weary in their daily battles for the Lord, find in Philemon the refreshment and rest needed to regain strength for renewed warfare. The phrase 'my brother' (the word 'my' is not in the Greek, but adding it indicates the affectionate tone conveyed by the position of the word 'brother' in the sentence) suggests that Paul sees in this ministry of Philemon something attractive and compelling, which binds the apostle and the local Christian leader together in a special bond. It is because of who Philemon already is that Paul can now appeal: refresh *my* heart in Christ (v.20, on which see the notes).

III. THE REQUEST (8–22)

The subtlety of the letter now becomes apparent. Paul is not writing in order to suggest, far less to enforce, a law or rule of conduct. Rather, he moves through an almost bewildering series of *identifications*. (a) Beginning by claiming Philemon and Apphia as his brother and sister (v.1), and giving to Philemon in particular the description 'beloved' and the title 'co-worker', he identifies fully with him in verses 4–7: Philemon's love makes him glad and grateful. To this point he will return (v.20). In the mean time, he notes Philemon's love for 'all the saints' (vv.4, 7), and prays that this will have its full effect (v.6). (b) He then turns round and identifies himself with Onesimus. He is 'my son' (v.10), 'my very heart' (v.12), 'very dear to me' (v.16); and Paul will take responsibility for his debts (vv.18–19). Even while he is making this second identification, Paul is hinting at the conclusion of the syllogism. (c) He assumes that Philemon would like to be able to help in his captivity, but Onesimus has been standing in for him, *representing* him (v.13; *cf*. Phil. 2:30). This is possible because Onesimus and Philemon are, though they do not realize it, 'dear brothers' to one another (v.16). (d) He then draws the conclusion proper: the welcome you would afford to *me* must be given to *him*, and the debts you would have put on *his* bill belong on *mine* instead (vv.17–19). Philemon and Onesimus are, in fact, in the same boat: both are debtors – to Paul (v.19). The wheel thus comes full circle: if Philemon has a reputation for refreshing the hearts of the saints (v.7), let him now refresh Paul's too (v.20). Philemon and Onesimus are to be united – in Paul. The apostle, so to speak, plays Christ to them, his ministry of reconciliation mirroring that of Christ at every point (2 Cor. 5:17–21).

A. ONESIMUS AND PAUL (8–16)

The first section of the appeal focuses primarily on Onesimus himself ('I appeal to you for my son Onesimus', v.10). It consists of five short sections: the basis of Paul's right to make the appeal (vv.8–9), the appeal itself (v.10), Onesimus' new character (vv.11–12), Paul's reasons for sending him back instead of keeping him (vv.13–14) and a suggestion as to God's purpose in allowing the whole sequence of events to come about (vv.15–16). Two things are emphasized throughout: the close bond between Paul and Onesimus, and the love which Paul hopes to awaken in Philemon towards his erstwhile slave. From here Paul will be able to draw his conclusions ('therefore . . .', v.17).

8. Paul has thanked God for Philemon's love, and it is to love, not duty (*therefore*), that he will now appeal. By saying *although in Christ I could be bold and order you to do what you ought to do*, he indicates that he is not denying the fact that as an apostle he has certain rights. He knows, however, that to use them in this case would be inappropriate. Merely obeying an order would not necessarily elicit from Philemon that increase in understanding and love for which Paul has prayed (v.6). At the same time, he is indeed hinting that there is something which Philemon 'ought to do' ('your duty', JB, NEB), even while saying, in effect, 'but I shan't mention that' (compare the rhetorical device in v.19).

9. Instead, Paul knows that there is a more excellent way. *I appeal to you on the basis of love*. Behind this choice of the right sort of appeal lies an all-important point: living Christianly makes people more human, not less. No Christian should grumble at extra demands of love. They are golden opportunities to draw on the reserves of divine love, and in so doing to become more fully oneself in Christ, more completely in the image of God, more authentically human. It is not merely Onesimus for whom Paul is here pastorally concerned.

Philemon's love for Paul is to be rekindled as he thinks of the paradoxical offices the apostle holds. *I then, as Paul – an old man and now also a prisoner* . . . It is more likely that for 'old man' we should read 'ambassador'. The two Greek words involved (*presbutēs* and *presbeutēs*) are not only virtually identical in spelling and punctuation: they are frequently interchangeable (see Lightfoot, pp.338f.), and the very similar collocation of ideas in 2 Corinthians 5:20 and Ephesians 6:19–20 strongly support the reading 'ambassador'. (It is not clear, in addition, that Paul was now particularly elderly or that, even if he were, it would make much sense in the present context for this to be made the basis of an appeal to one who might well be around the same age.)

To call himself an 'ambassador', however, and then to use the word 'prisoner' (as in v.1) as a further title, characteristically paradoxical in its command of respect, might look as though he

were intending after all to issue orders to Philemon instead of
appealing on the basis of love. One way out of this dilemma is to
see the clause as concessive: these are the rights which Paul has,
but of which he is not going to make use (so Caird). But it is
more satisfactory to let the weight of the sentence fall on the
phrase which qualifies both 'prisoner' and (I think, though
grammatically this must remain uncertain) 'ambassador', *i.e. of
Christ Jesus*. Paul is treading a recognizable path, which will
reach its goal in verses 17–19. If it is as *Christ's* ambassador, and
prisoner, that he is writing, then the appropriate method for
him to use is that of Christ himself, namely, the setting aside of
rights in order to bring salvation to others (see Phil. 2:1–11;
3:2–11).[1] The sentence then goes both with what precedes and
with what follows: 'for love's sake I choose to appeal to you,
since my real identity is that of Paul, the Ambassador (and now,[2]
moreover, the Prisoner), not of some haughty monarch whose
arrogance I must ape, but of Christ Jesus, whose authority is
exercised from the cross.'

10. Paul now builds on this foundation. *I appeal to you for my
son Onesimus.* The delay in naming Onesimus has suggested to
some that Paul is waiting until he has said as many good things
about him as possible. This may be so, but Philemon surely
knew as soon as anyone that his ex-slave had returned. The
important point is that Onesimus has come back not so much as
a slave but as a son.[3] The Rabbis used the metaphor of sonship
to describe the teacher-pupil relationship: Paul was fond of
using it for that between himself and his converts (1 Cor.
4:14–15; 2 Cor. 6:13; Gal. 4:19; Phil. 2:22; *cf.* 1 Tim. 1:2, *etc.*). A
new birth has taken place within the slave: he *became my son
while I was in chains*, or, closer to the Greek, 'whose father I have
become in my imprisonment' (RSV). The name 'Onesimus' literally means 'useful', deriving from the same root as the phrase
'have some benefit' in verse 20. It was a common slave's name,
starting most likely as a nickname. The sentence could be taken

---

[1] This overcomes, *e.g.*, Lohse's objection (p.199) to the translation 'ambassador' on the
grounds that Paul is not appealing to his office or rank.
[2] A reference, perhaps, to the recent nature of the imprisonment: see Martin, p.163.
[3] See Gal. 4:1–7; *cf.* Lk. 15:19–24.

to emphasize this, so as to say 'whom I have begotten as "Onesimus" ', *i.e.* who has become really 'useful' at last through his new 'birth': but this seems to over-anticipate the following verse. Conversely, the idea that 'Onesimus' was the slave's 'Christian' name, given in baptism, is unlikely; it would greatly reduce the effect of the word-play that is about to come. The best way to take the verse is to say that Paul is appealing concerning (not simply 'for', in the sense of asking for him to be sent back) the slave Onesimus, who has become, like so many, a 'child' of Paul, through becoming, under his ministry, a child of God.

11. Paul now exploits this meaning of Onesimus' name: *Formerly he was useless to you, but now he has become useful.* The words 'useless' and 'useful' are even closer in the Greek than in the English (*achrēstos* and *euchrēstos*: the latter is actually emphatic, 'really useful', *i.e.* not just in name). Such puns were common in ancient literature.[1] In addition, the underlying word *chrēstos* was indistinguishable in pronunciation from the title *Christos*,[2] so that there may be a double pun intended. Onesimus is now in Christ. And if he is *euchrēstos*, Christian and 'useful', that means that his relationship with Philemon, and not just with Paul, will be seen in quite a new light. He will be 'Onesimus', 'useful', *both to you and to me.*

12-13. *I am sending him* (the Greek is literally 'I sent', since Paul here, as in Col. 4:8, writes as though speaking at the moment when Philemon is reading the letter) *back to you.* The verb could be a veiled judicial metaphor, 'I am referring his case to you': certainly Philemon has, legally, the final say. But if so the tone is ironic, since Paul is certainly not implying that he cannot make up his own mind as to what should be done.[3] Far

---

[1] For other examples, see O'Brien, pp.291 f.; Lohse, p.200.

[2] See Bruce, *Paul*, pp.381 f., discussing the famous text in Suetonius, *Life of Claudius* 25:4.

[3] It has sometimes been thought (see *e.g.* Bruce, *Paul*, pp.399 f.) that Paul is attempting here to implement the Old Testament laws regarding slaves (Dt. 23:15-16, *etc.*), but this seems to me unlikely. It is true that there are echoes of similar ideas here to those found in the Old Testament provisions (see on v.15 below), but this would be an uncharacteristic way for Paul to use the Old Testament. Its commands, in this respect at least, relate to the era of the Mosaic covenant, designed for the time when the people of God were a single racial entity, which they are now no longer (Gal. 3:19-22).

from it: Onesimus *is my very heart*. The word here translated 'heart' ties together the three movements of the letter: Philemon has refreshed the hearts of the saints (v.7), Onesimus is Paul's 'very heart', and Paul will ask Philemon (v.20) to refresh *his* heart too. This verse, and indeed the whole epistle, is a reminder of how totally misguided is that picture of Paul which sees him as a hard-headed, unattractive, dogmatic thinker. He was clearly capable, and not afraid, of forming deep and satisfying friendships. As a result, he says, *I would have liked to keep him with me*, even if it meant harbouring a runaway slave, *so that he could take your place in helping me while I am in chains for the gospel*. As so often with a good piece of writing, the power lies in that which is implied but not stated. Paul takes for granted two vital points. First, he (Philemon) would have wanted to help Paul while in prison, had not other duties made that impossible. Second, Onesimus will serve very nicely as Philemon's representative and hence substitute. The identity (*koinōnia* again) between them as master and slave makes Onesimus' service peculiarly appropriate, and enables Paul to credit his master for his work. (*Cf.* 1 Cor. 16:17; Phil. 2:30; 4:18.) If Philemon concedes these points, the game is over. Even though in prison, Paul is the mid-point between the estranged pair.

14. As Paul gave up his rights (vv.8–9), so he now gives up his preferences: *But I did not want to do anything without your consent*. The aorist 'I did not want' refers to a single action of the will, contrasting with the previous imperfect 'I was contemplating . . .'. This statement does not imply that Paul is asking Philemon to return Onesimus to him. All that the Greek means is that Paul wished to take no action without having Philemon in on the discussion. This is *so that any favour you do will be spontuneous and not forced*.[1] 'Any favour you do' is potentially misleading: Paul does not want 'favours', but, literally, 'your good thing', which ties this phrase to 'every good thing' in verse 6. Philemon must do what is 'good' in the situation. But Paul wants him to be in on the decision-making process. When God is at work, all the actors in the drama are important. The word

[1]See the partial parallel in the letter of Pliny already discussed (9:21): *vereor ne videar non rogare sed cogere*, 'I'm afraid you will think I am using pressure, not persuasion' (tr. Radice).

here translated 'spontaneous' does not mean that the action has not been carefully thought out, but rather indicates that the person concerned has reached a settled conviction on a subject and is happy to carry it through. It is the opposite not of 'premeditated' but of 'unwilling'.

Paul therefore couchès his appeal in language which exerts no external, belittling compulsion. It creates, instead, a new context within which Philemon can *understand* the situation from God's point of view (see v.6, once more) and so can begin to desire the good for himself. To assist someone in reaching what must remain his own decision is not to enslave him, but to set him free. This is the nature of Paul's authority 'in Christ': it is a healing, creative responsibility which, by setting out the facts of the case, theologically, practically and pastorally, invites Christians to work out the proper conclusions in belief and practice. Perhaps Paul is thus once more dropping very gentle hints over and above what he actually says. Consider, he seems to be saying, how different it feels to be treated like a human being instead of as an unthinking piece of property . . .

15. In this process, of attempting to understand a situation from God's point of view and so responding to it in a Christian fashion, there is always room for restrained speculation about the providential purpose that may underlie curious events. If it is true that 'in all things God works for the good of those who love him' (Rom. 8:28), it is also true that Christians are sometimes, and to a limited extent, privileged to catch a glimpse of how this is being accomplished. The *perhaps* at the start of the verse is the necessary qualification for all such claims: they remain a matter of faith, not sight. So Paul may be suggesting, in a typically oblique way, that God may have intended Onesimus to run away[1] so that he might find Christ for himself – instead, 'perhaps', of picking up a second-hand faith, or the outward trappings of Christianity, in his master's house. Perhaps, then, *the reason he was separated from you for a little while was*

---

[1] This is to take 'he was separated' in its full passive sense, indicating divine action: the 'perhaps' and the 'so that' strongly support this interpretation over the alternative (grammatically possible though it may be) which takes the verb in an active sense, simply meaning 'he went away'.

that you might have him back for good. Readers of the letter since at least Chrysostom in the fourth century AD have been struck by the parallel with Joseph's gracious handling of his brothers in Egypt: 'you intended to harm me, but God intended it for good' (Gn. 50:20). Joseph, like Paul, held a steady belief in God's providential overruling of human sin and folly. Patience and forgiveness grow well in soil like that.

But in what sense will Philemon 'have him back for good'? The word translated 'for good' could have a mainly 'spiritual' connotation: to all eternity Philemon and Onesimus will be brothers in Christ. But if that is all Paul had intended, he need not have sent Onesimus back at all. Tychicus could have taken a rather different note to Philemon, Onesimus could have stayed with Paul, and a theoretical 'reconciliation' could have taken place. But that is simply not good enough. The closing phrase of the next verse (literally, 'in the flesh and in the Lord') indicates, rather, that *aiōnion* is intended to carry both its senses: 'for all eternity' and 'permanently'.[1] It may indeed be that verse 21 hints at a different eventual outcome: but Philemon has at least to be *prepared* to welcome Onesimus back on a permanent basis. Significantly, too, Onesimus (like the prodigal son) must be prepared to go back on those terms. To exchange greetings, keep up appearances for a few days, and then part once more would not be real reconciliation.

16. God may, then, be intending that Philemon have Onesimus back *no longer as a slave, but better than a slave, as a dear brother.* This is not a request for emancipation. It simply applies what is said about relations between Christian masters and slaves in, *e.g.*, 1 Corinthians 7:22 or Colossians 3:22 – 4:1. Even if Onesimus returns to his post, he can never again be merely a slave, a walking household utility. *He is very dear to me but even dearer to you.* Paul does not actually repeat the word 'dear'. It looks as though he first intends to stop at 'a brother beloved': *that* is how Philemon is to treat Onesimus. He then amplifies

---

[1] This is the one point (see n.3, p.182, above) where the language of the Old Testament law relating to slaves almost certainly shows through: in Ex. 21:6 a slave who rejects the offer of freedom and opts to stay with his master is bound to do so 'for ever' (*eis ton aiōna*, LXX).

this, adding 'particularly to me'; Philemon must treat Onesimus as a brother beloved to *Paul*; then, changing direction again, he takes the extra step which will bring him within a stone's throw of the final imperatives of verses 17 and 18: 'but how much more to you'. This may seem odd: Paul and Onesimus had begun their relationship on the right foot, but Philemon had reason to be angry with his former slave. But Paul means what he says. To have a member of one's household (even a previously useless one) turning to Christ is a greater cause for joy than the conversion of a stranger. Second, Onesimus really is a 'brother' to Philemon, in that both of them (vv.10, 19) have Paul as their parent 'in the Lord'. Onesimus, then, will be dear to Philemon *both as a man and as a brother in the Lord*, or, as RSV more literally translates, 'both in the flesh and in the Lord'.

B. ONESIMUS AND PHILEMON (17–22)

There being no further risk that Philemon will think that Paul is putting him in a false position, the appeal can be put in plain terms, with four straight imperatives: welcome Onesimus, put his debts on my bill, refresh my heart in the Lord – and (by the way) make up the bed for me in the spare room. Here, at the climax of the letter, we witness nothing less than the radical application of the doctrine of justification to everyday living. No Christian has a right to refuse a welcome to one whom God has welcomed. Faith in Christ, the basis of justification, is the basis also of *koinōnia*. Justification by faith must result in fellowship by faith.[1] This latter means the settled determination to share fully in mutual fellowship with all those who share the faith, however awkward or angular or muddled or misguided, or simply *different*, they may be, or appear to be.[2]

At the basis of both justification and fellowship there is what Luther called the 'wondrous exchange'. Paul's 'ministry of reconciliation', according to 2 Corinthians 5:17–21, centres upon

---

[1] See the Greek of v.6 (*koinōnia tēs pisteōs sou*), literally 'the fellowship of your faith'. Compare the other great 'welcome' passage in Paul (Rom. 14:1 – 15:13).
[2] Calvin's comment (p.399) is worth quoting: 'It would be a sign of haughty pride, if he should be ashamed to count as his brother those whom God numbers among his sons.'

the awesome statement: 'God was in Christ reconciling the world to himself, not counting their trespasses against them, and entrusting to us the message of reconciliation . . . For our sake he made him to be sin who knew no sin, so that in him we might become the righteousness of God' (5:19, 21, RSV). What we find in the letter to Philemon as a whole is the extraordinary, and almost shocking, fact that Paul is reconciling master and slave by taking on himself the role of Christ. For Onesimus' sake God makes Paul a debtor to Philemon (even though he owes him nothing), so that in Paul Onesimus may find a welcome into the church and home where he now truly belongs. God is in Paul reconciling Philemon and Onesimus. This is the Christ-shaped ministry of which Paul wrote in Colossians 1:24–29.

17–18. So, Paul can now conclude, *if you consider me a partner, welcome him as you would welcome me.* The word for 'partner' here is *koinōnos*: not a 'partner' in business merely, but one who shares the *koinōnia* of verse 6 (on which see the notes). Paul is now on firm ground: Philemon will not refuse to acknowledge Paul as a *koinōnos*, but if he takes Paul he will (because of vv.8–16) inevitably get Onesimus as well. If the slave has stood in for the master by helping Paul in prison (v.13), he must now stand in for Paul by visiting Paul's friend, and by receiving on the apostle's behalf the welcome which he is temporarily and unavoidably unable to accept in person. And, so that Paul can be quite sure that Onesimus will have his (Paul's) 'righteousness' in Philemon's eyes, he will assume responsibility for Onesimus' sins: *If he has done you any wrong or owes you anything, charge it to me.* It is impossible to say for certain whether Paul refers to theft on Onesimus' part. But it would be very odd to say what he does if he knew that Philemon had no grounds for complaint, or even if he were simply unsure about the matter. *Qui s'excuse s'accuse.* It seems likely, then, that the young slave had stolen from his master in order to provide for himself at least until he could get to the city.[1] From Philemon's point of

---

[1] Houlden (p.226) strangely attempts to play this down, implying that Onesimus' offence was minor and that Philemon was 'a rather fiery character' who would take unnecessary offence at small peccadilloes. The more usual view seems altogether preferable in the context: see below.

view, this was probably the most hurtful part of the whole business; and Paul, having cushioned it on all sides so as to cause minimum pain, deals with it in such a way as to effect speediest healing. Onesimus' debts are to be put in the ledger under Paul's name: and there they will find that they are more than cancelled out. They disappear as totally as the sins placed to Christ's account on the cross.

19. Paul reinforces the point with an ironic IOU note: *I, Paul, am writing this with my own hand. I will pay it back.* Whether Paul has here taken the pen from the secretary for the first time (see on Col. 4:18), or whether this verse indicates that he has written this very personal letter all in his own hand, it is impossible to say, though I incline towards the latter view. The important thing is that the really difficult request, that Philemon forgive the actual wrong done to him, is made not only by a beautiful and delicate argument but also in the right tone of voice. There is nothing heavy-handed about it. However mixed Philemon's feelings may have been at verse 18, his lips must have twitched as he read on to verse 19 and saw how gently and yet effectively he was being teased: *not to mention that you owe me your very self.* As in verse 8, Paul uses the rhetorician's transparent trick of declaring that he will not mention something, thereby of course mentioning it (compare 2 Cor. 9:4). It is this verse that tells us that Philemon had, like Onesimus, become a Christian under Paul's ministry. He therefore owes Paul his own very self: the true self which he had found, and become, in becoming Christ's.[1] And this 'debt' will more than outweigh any material debts Paul may have incurred by taking on Onesimus' overdraft.

20. The gentle irony continues. If it is a matter of debts, then Paul has a right to claim a dividend on his investment in Philemon: *I do wish, brother, that I may have some benefit from you in the Lord.* This translation scarcely catches the mood of the Greek, which might perhaps be expressed: 'Yes, my dear man –now I come to think of it, *I* want some return from *you!*' The word for

[1]See Williams, p.188.

'benefit' is *onaimēn*, cognate with *Onēsimos*, and the whole tone of the passage, backed up by the word-play of verse 11, strongly suggests that the pun is again deliberate. It is now Philemon's turn to be 'useful' to Paul – by doing for Paul what he is apparently good at doing for everybody else (v.7):[1] *refresh my heart in Christ.* The 'my' is emphatic in the Greek: it is now *my* turn to be refreshed. How? By Philemon welcoming (not Paul, but) Onesimus: the principle of *koinōnia* is at work still.

21. It may be more gentle rhetoric, but Paul probably knows Philemon well enough to mean it in all sincerity: *Confident of your obedience, I write to you* (literally, 'I wrote': see on v.12, above). 'Obedience', a more flexible word in Greek than in English, does not mean that Paul has after all been issuing orders. Paul regularly uses the word to indicate the total response of the whole person to the summons of God in the gospel (Rom. 1:5; 6:16; 15:18; 16:19, 26; 2 Cor. 7:15; 10:5–6).[2] Paul has not asked Philemon for blind obedience. He has given him the gospel, incarnated in a new way but still clearly recognizable. The 'obedience' he seeks is Philemon's heartfelt response to the call of love. And, if he can be confident here, he can be certain that love, once awakened, will go the second mile: *knowing that you will do even more than I ask.* This 'even more' raises, of course, the question with which Paul, having teased Philemon, now teases his modern readers. I have suggested above (pp.167f.) what seems to me the most likely answer. Although the main aim of the letter is the permanent reconciliation of master and slave, the 'even more' may hint at a second purpose: perhaps Philemon will be willing to emancipate Onesimus, if not immediately, then when Paul comes to stay (v.22). Perhaps, if Philippians (see 2:24) comes from this same imprisonment, Paul will soon be on his way to Philippi, and is hoping that Onesimus will be allowed to accompany him.

[1]This parallel makes it very unlikely that we should translate, with NEB, 'relieve my anxiety'.
[2]This, with our present passage, is the complete list of all Paul's uses of 'obedience', with the exception of the reference to *Christ's* obedience in Rom. 5:19. The cognate verb 'obey' is used similarly in, *e.g.*, Rom. 10:16.

22. *And one thing more* – almost 'oh, and by the way . . .'. In keeping with the tone throughout, Paul refers almost casually to the vital follow-up visit: *prepare a guest room* (the word can mean 'hospitality' in general, but it is almost universally agreed that it here refers to lodging, not board) *for me.* We find a similar theme in 1 Corinthians 4:18–21; 2 Corinthians 12:14; 13:1–3, the difference being that, while the Corinthian church needed the iron fist, Philemon needs only the kid glove. A word to the wise is sufficient. Paul's planned visit is not a threat ('so make sure that my instructions are carried out, or else') so much as a promise: *because I hope to be restored to you in answer to your prayers.* Paul has been praying for Philemon (vv.4–7); now it appears that, as befits fellow-members of the *koinōnia*, Philemon and his household have also been praying for Paul. 'Restored' is not quite right: Paul had never been to Colosse in the first place (Col. 2:1). The Greek simply means 'granted', 'given as a gift', the root being *charis*, 'grace'. Philemon's church, having prayed for Paul's release, will experience it as a gift of grace. And if they have been praying along these lines they will scarcely be hostile to the letter Paul has now written. They and he are bound together in Christian *koinōnia*, undergirded with mutual prayer.

Paul's projected visit to Colosse is one of the stronger arguments for locating the prison epistles, and particularly Philemon, in Ephesus (see the Introduction to Colossians, pp.34ff., above). Paul went to Rome 'having no further scope' in the Western Mediterranean, and with the full intention of going on to Spain (Rom. 15:23–24, 28). Even if Paul was writing from Rome, having completely changed his mind about his vocation and having decided to return to Asia Minor after all, he would doubtless have had many other calls to make, not least in Ephesus itself,[1] and would scarcely expect to arrive in Colosse for a month or two, at the very lowest estimate, from the time of his release. Philemon's guest-room would not need preparing until Paul could write from the nearest large town: say, from

---

[1] To whose church leaders he had, according to Acts 20:25 and 38, solemnly declared that they would never see his face again. Even if this passage were to be judged non-historical, it seems unlikely that its author would have written this had he known of a subsequent trip to Asia Minor. It could of course be argued that Paul intended to make such a trip but was prevented, but this would be to pile one guess on top of another.

Ephesus. Similar arguments could be employed against the theory of a Caesarean imprisonment as the place of writing: by that period, Paul already had his sights on Rome, and Spain beyond that (see above), and would scarcely have time for visits *en route* to all the small-town churches in Asia Minor.

IV. CLOSING GREETINGS (23-25)

23-24. It is natural that at the head of the list of greetings (on which see the commentary on Col. 4:10-14) should come *Epaphras*; himself a Colossian (Col. 4:12), he had preached the gospel to his fellow-townspeople in the first place (Col. 1:7-8) and was now back in Ephesus with Paul, as a *fellow prisoner for Christ Jesus*. Whether this 'imprisonment' is to be taken literally or metaphorically it is impossible to say for certain. A possible clue, which might suggest that it is metaphorical, may be found in the fact that the word used is not cognate with the root translated 'prisoner' in verses 1, 9 and 'chains' in verses 10, 13, but is, as in Colossians 4:10, 'fellow-prisoner-of-war'. The following phrase is, literally, 'in Christ Jesus', not 'of Christ Jesus' as in verse 1. As in the case of Aristarchus in Colossians, I am inclined to think that Epaphras is a literal prisoner, like Paul, in the battle between Christ and the powers of the present age.

Epaphras, then, *sends you greetings. And so do Mark, Aristarchus, Demas and Luke, my fellow-workers.* This list is virtually identical with that in the parallel passage in Colossians. The one exception is that Jesus Justus is missing from the present roll-call. It has been suggested, with some ingenuity, that he is present after all, disguised as the 'Jesus' in the phrase 'Christ Jesus': in the Greek the word-order is 'Epaphras sends you greetings, my fellow-captive in Christ Jesus, Mark, Aristarchus', *etc.* Only one letter would need to be changed in the manuscript for us to punctuate '. . . in Christ, Jesus, Mark . . .', but it still seems a little unlikely that Paul would have left such a possible ambiguity so wide open. Equally unlikely is the suggestion that Jesus Justus is not mentioned because he would not be known in Colosse: the same would almost certainly be true of many others on the list, and it did not prevent Paul mentioning him in

Colossians 4:11. Perhaps this Jesus, although with Paul the day that Colossians was dictated, simply happened to be absent during the writing of the letter to Philemon. For the other names on the list, all of them classed as 'fellow-workers', see the commentary on Colossians 4:10–14.

25. The conventional tone of the closing greeting, once again, should not blind us to the truth it conveys to us, and the power that the expressed prayer conveyed to Philemon. It is a hard thing Paul has asked of him: a superhuman task of heartfelt reconciliation and forgiveness. If he is to do it without pride or anger, he cannot do it without grace. But grace is what is available: *the grace of the Lord Jesus Christ*, who, though he was rich, yet for our sake became poor, that we by his poverty might become rich (2 Cor. 8:9); the same Christ who took upon himself the nature, and the death, of the slave (Phil. 2:7–8). This Christ-shaped grace has informed Paul's whole understanding of *koinōnia*, which has in turn dominated the whole letter. It is this same grace that is now to *be with your spirit*: to be let loose, by Paul's prayers and words, in Philemon's life, to make his home, and the church that meets there, the scene of a reconciliation that will prove beyond any doubt that the gospel of Jesus Christ is not a matter of talk, but of power.